T0290549

Case Studies in Cultural Entrepreneurship

Case Studies in Cultural Entrepreneurship

How to Create Relevant and Sustainable Institutions

Edited by Gretchen Sullivan Sorin and Lynne A. Sessions

ROWMAN & LITTLEFIELD
Lanham • Boulder • New York • London

Published by Rowman & Littlefield
A wholly owned subsidiary of The Rowman & Littlefield Publishing Group, Inc.
4501 Forbes Boulevard, Suite 200, Lanham, Maryland 20706
www.rowman.com

Unit A, Whitacre Mews, 26-34 Stannary Street, London SE11 4AB

British Library Cataloguing in Publication Information Available

Library of Congress Cataloging-in-Publication Data

Case studies in cultural entrepreneurship : how to create relevant and sustainable institutions / [edited by] Gretchen Sorin and Lynne A. Sessions.
pages cm
Includes bibliographical references and index.
ISBN 978-1-4422-3007-1 (cloth : alkaline paper) — ISBN 978-1-4422-3008-8 (paperback : alkaline paper) — ISBN 978-1-4422-3009-5 (electronic)
1. Museums—United States—Management—Case studies. 2. Museums—Canada—Management—Case studies. 3. Cultural property—United States—Management—Case studies. 4. Cultural property—Canada—Management—Case studies. 5. Entrepreneurship—United States—Case studies. 6. Entrepreneurship—Canada—Case studies. 7. Sustainability—United States—Case studies. 8. Sustainability—Canada—Case studies. I. Sorin, Gretchen Sullivan. II. Sessions, Lynne A., 1955–
AM11.C37 2015
069'.0680973—dc23
2014047409

∞ ™ The paper used in this publication meets the minimum requirements of American National Standard for Information Sciences Permanence of Paper for Printed Library Materials, ANSI/NISO Z39.48-1992.

Printed in the United States of America

For Alan and Martin
and
For cultural entrepreneurs, past, present, and future

Contents

Preface

Gretchen Sullivan Sorin and Lynne A. Sessions

A cultural entrepreneur: A risk taker who can lead fundamental organizational change through powerful ideas and creative solutions.

When it is so easy to access information on the Internet, what makes a museum visit exciting? With so many activities competing for leisure time, why would anyone visit a static historic house? Museums and other cultural institutions now operate in complex, turbulent environments. For example, technological innovation has fundamentally changed how people take in information, communicate, and think. Information flows freely, 24/7, to be digested in 140 characters, 10-second sound bites, and 6-second videos. Immediate response and gratification are the norm. Indeed, why would someone visit a static historic house?

Technological innovations have also changed philanthropy. Money flows as freely as information, making it easier for individuals to donate while at the same time creating greater competition for donations. Today's donor views his or her donation as an investment and wants to know how the money is being spent and what will be received in return. The world has become both smaller and bigger, and complex technological, social, and economic forces are and have been drastically reshaping the role of the museum in contemporary life. For many cultural organizations, those with wealthy benefactors and those struggling to survive, keeping up is hard to do.

This is the environment in which the entrepreneur thrives, finding opportunities in change, taking calculated risks, and creating organizational infrastructures that not only quickly respond to change but are an integral part of the opportunity discovery process. Entrepreneurs and entrepreneurial organizations have long been a celebrated part of the for-profit world. However, it is only recently that in the search for relevancy and sustainability, not-for-profit cultural institutions have begun to embrace entrepreneurial thinking. So how does a cultural institution become relevant and sustainable? It is one thing to simply say "apply entrepreneurial models to your organization." It is quite another to find those ideas that make cultural organizations central to their communities. To demonstrate, let's start by asking what would a relevant, sustainable cultural organization look like if it, like Athena,[1] were born fully formed?

In this ideal organization, leadership is entrepreneurial and opportunity focused and clearly communicates the organizational vision. Boards of directors are active, capable, and supportive and work as a team with organizational leadership, staff, and volunteers. The organization is fully staffed and its structure is flexible enough to identify and embrace opportunities at all levels. Sufficient resources exist to allow for active, ongoing strategic planning, research, and experimentation. Reimagination of the organization's purpose occurs on a regular basis. Leadership, staff, and board fully embrace this vision and process and as a result, the organization is an integral part of and responsive to a variety of communities of stakeholders. Sustainability through relevance is assured!

Just about now, you are probably saying, "If I had all of those things in my organization, I wouldn't need this book!" And we might agree; however, in our experience, the extent to which these ideal attributes exist in not-for-profit cultural organizations varies considerably. The good news is that through effective leadership and creative problem solving, organizations can develop these attributes, and entrepreneurship and business skills training can help to develop effective leaders. It is exactly this perspective that led to the creation of the Institute for Cultural Entrepreneurship (ICE) and ultimately to *Case Studies in Cultural Entrepreneurship: How to Create Relevant and Sustainable Institutions.*

INSTITUTE FOR CULTURAL ENTREPRENEURSHIP (ICE)

Concerned about declining museum visitation, changing demographics, and challenges to leadership, the Cooperstown Graduate Program in Museum Studies (CGP), the Museum Association of New York (MANY), and the New York State Historical Association (NYSHA) partnered to develop a mid-career training program to reenergize museum professionals and to train and develop cultural entrepreneurs, risk takers who could lead future organizational change through powerful ideas and creative solutions. The Institute for Cultural Entrepreneurship (ICE), originally funded by the Institute of Museum and Library Services, began in 2008 as a four-day on-site program that combined business training with creativity exercises and case studies of successful entrepreneurial institutions.

For years, the Cooperstown Graduate Program has been expanding business and creativity training for students. Our interviews with successful museum directors indicated that museums today look for applicants with both museum experience and skills that go well beyond collections care and management. Business skills, fund-raising, project management, strategic planning, marketing, and most importantly, creative thinking and problem solving are key skills for success. In an effort to explore methods of providing mid-career professionals with new ideas and successful business practices, ICE was born.

In the 1960s, the emerging field of museum studies focused on the academic disciplines of history, art history, and anthropology, with the addition of collections care and, later, educational program development. These training programs helped to professionalize the museum field and to manage museum collections, but their academic focus has not necessarily kept pace with the changing leadership skill sets of museum directors who must lead not-for-profit businesses. Since the 1980s, the focus of some programs shifted away from object-based learning, expanding to include visitor services, diversification of museum audiences, economic innovation, and assessing effectiveness. While these skills are being included in museum studies curricula for entry-level students, mid-career professionals—those who are soon to inherit the mantle of museum leadership—may not have had the opportunity to spend time learning these skills.

Over the past few years, CGP and MANY have sought to discover which attributes innovative museum leaders share, to discern how museums may be affected by the loss of senior museum leaders, and to identify mid-career individuals who are eager to learn leadership skills as they transition into senior administrative and programmatic positions. Specifically, three sets of data were analyzed to better understand the needs of mid-career museum professionals. First, a 2004 CGP survey with museum leaders identified the skills that twenty-first-century museum professionals must have. The survey was designed by a social scientist and included in-depth interviews with twenty-one innovative leaders from around the country, who were asked to define the requisite knowledge and skills needed by entry-level professionals to be successful and to rise to leadership positions in museums. The key informants were selected based on conversations with staff at the American Alliance of Museums (AAM) and the American Association for State and Local History (AASLH) and represented a variety of museum sizes, disciplines, and geographic locations. The results of this survey were published in the autumn 2004 issue of *History News*.[2] In 2006, based on the data gathered within the state, MANY published a white paper, "Who's Next: Questioning the Future of Museum Leadership in New York State," written by Joan H. Baldwin.

Second, open discussions were held in Rochester, Albany, and New York with professionals at all levels within the field, including CEOs, directors, and senior staff members from twelve museums and historical societies, as well as graduate students and faculty from five of the state's nine museum studies programs. Several individuals who had left the field and key staff people from the New York State Council on the Arts were present. The most significant finding from these meetings showed that mid-career training was a recurring theme in all three regional discussions. Participants felt it was an unaddressed need. Too few organizations place value on leadership training, failing to recognize that these experiences have a ripple effect that ultimately benefits the organization. Apart from the obvious benefits of providing new knowledge, mid-career education gives participants mentors and a peer group. Finally, in 2007 CGP and MANY conducted a survey of mid-career professionals to help us shape the on-site program.

As a part of the development of a curriculum on cultural entrepreneurship, we collected case studies of institutions and institutional leaders who have developed entrepreneurial approaches to problem solving. The case study approach to learning, pioneered by Harvard University in the 1920s, is routinely used in business schools and institutes throughout the world but is far less commonly used in training museum professionals. We wanted to correct that deficiency. Case studies detail real-life problems and decisions that take place within a well-described context developed from multiple sources of data such as organizational records, interviews with key actors, media reports, and in some instances, direct participation in the events. The reader has access to the complexity of the situation facing these leaders. Historical background, choices, actors, external and internal forces, decision points, and results are detailed as they occur over time.

ORGANIZATION OF THE BOOK

Five of these cases are included in this book. Through demonstrating how cultural entrepreneurship in complex environments drives organizational change, these readable cases offer an in-depth look at how leaders in a variety of cultural organizations—small and large; local, regional, and national; domestic and foreign; museums and arts organizations alike—found opportunities in complex situations to create new identities and missions and, in doing so, revitalized their organizations and in many cases their surrounding communities.

Chapter 1, written by Cooperstown Graduate Program director and Distinguished Professor Gretchen Sullivan Sorin, examines how the Centre d'histoire de Montréal redefined its mission from that of a tourist welcome center focusing on the city's built heritage to showcasing the voices and memories of the people of Montreal. In doing so, the Centre d'histoire de Montréal carved out a unique niche among competing museums and attracted new visitors to the museum.

Chapter 2, "The Weeksville Heritage Center," written by former Weeksville executive director Pamela Green, details the forty-year journey of rediscovery, preservation, and expansion of Weeksville, the first free, independent black community in the country. Located in one of New York City's poorest neighborhoods and subject to a number of environmental shocks that severely affected funding and, by extension, the preservation process, the Weeksville Heritage Center found success through extending the definition of community that defined Weeksville to the current-day community surrounding the historic site. By engaging the local stakeholders as well as citywide supporters, the Weeksville Heritage Center gained relevancy and sustainability.

Chapter 3 introduces an arts organization to the case mix. In the 1970s, Proctors Theatre, a former vaudeville house, was seized by the city of Schenectady for back taxes. Written by Nicholas DeMarco, the story of Proctors's transformation is the story of how entrepreneurial visionary Philip Morris and a proactive board turned this local not-for-profit arts and culture institution into a driving force for regional economic and community redevelopment and revitalization.

Community development and revitalization are also central themes in Jerome Enzler's "America's River: Reinvention of The Mississippi River Museum," found in chapter 4. From 1992 to 2003, the Dubuque County Historical Society and its Mississippi River Museum in Dubuque, Iowa, were part of a riverfront development effort called "America's River." Through vision, savvy development and fund-raising, and a focus on building critical local, regional, national, and federal partnerships, the Dubuque County Historical Society transformed into the nationally recognized Mississippi River Museum. Enzler's experiences as executive director for the Mississippi River Museum add detail and depth to this case.

Chapter 5 details the Strong's entrepreneurial journey from a struggling history and decorative arts museum with poor attendance to a museum of national caliber focused on the cultural history of play serving over a half-million visitors a year. As described by Amy Hollister Zarlengo, the Strong, located in Rochester, New York, and fueled by diligent strategic planning influenced by market research, created a flexible business culture and responsive operational structure that promoted innovation and creativity and allowed the institution to identify community needs and capitalize on opportunities.

Each case can stand on its own. (The notes and bibliography are contained within each case chapter.) But for those who wish to dig a little deeper into the cases as a whole, chapter 6, by Lynne Sessions, offers a discussion and analysis of the cases.

Ultimately, these cases show the entrepreneurial journeys taken as a variety of organizations worked to identify, adopt, and embrace new ways of thinking and acting. The cases can offer inspiration and ideas for practicing museum and other cultural organization professionals. Instructors can use this book as a companion piece for classroom and seminar instruction. Students who have not had substantive work experience in the field could benefit from the real-world examples. Professionals working for a variety of not-for-profit organizations may also find inspiration and ideas in these cases. Cultural organizations are not alone in facing turbulent environments and change. Relevancy and achieved sustainability through entrepreneurial action are relevant to all not-for-profit organizations. Above all, we encourage readers to discuss the cases with colleagues. What resonates with you? What do you see in your organization or what would you like to see? These conversations, framed around a common experience, can have immense value in shaping a shared vision and offering common language to help identify and implement entrepreneurial thinking and organizational change.

If we have learned anything, it is that everything changes and that we cannot always predict what will happen next. What is relevant will change. What is sustainable will change. It is only through ongoing feedback, research, trying new things, reflecting, and learning that the organization will achieve long-term relevancy and sustainability. There is a certain irony attached to the need of cultural institutions to learn to survive. For many years, museums dictated what the visitor experience should be, what the visitor should learn, and how the visitor should learn. Now, in order to be truly entrepreneurial organizations, museums themselves must be the students who embrace creativity, innovation, and a collective organizational questioning of the status quo.

For many years museum professionals have discussed and written about the need for a new generation of museum leaders who can adapt to new paradigms in museum work. We hope that *Case Studies in Cultural Entrepreneurship: How to Create Relevant and Sustainable Institutions* provides readers with a variety of ways to bring their institutions into the mainstream of their communities and offers inspiration for creative problem solving.

NOTES

1. In Greek mythology, Athena was born, fully clothed and armored, from the head of Zeus.

2. Gretchen Sullivan Sorin and Martin D. Sorin, "Museums, Professional Training and the Challenge of Leadership for the Future," *History News* 59, no. 4 (Autumn 2004).

Acknowledgments

We are indebted to the initial ICE planning team for shaping the project. Anne Ackerson, then director of the Museum Association of New York and an expert in museum leadership, and Gretchen Sorin, director of the Cooperstown Graduate Program, led the team that included a distinguished group: Philip Morris, director of Proctors Theatre, museum business consultant; Dorothy Chen-Courtin, president at Marketing & Management Associates for Non Profits; Rollie Adams, CEO of the Strong Museum; John Carnahan, retired visiting museum management professor at the Cooperstown Graduate Program; Joanne Curran, dean of Sage College of Albany and expert in education and creativity studies; Pam Green, executive director emerita of the Weeksville Heritage Society; Carol Ensecki, former president of the Brooklyn Children's Museum; and D. Stephen Elliott, director and CEO of the Minnesota Historical Society.

Pam Green, Nick DeMarco, Amy Hollister Zarlengo, and Jerry Enzler authored case studies, conducted detailed interviews with museum staff, and gathered a plethora of data on each institution. We are also especially grateful to Cate Bayles and Michelle Paulus for gathering photographs and other information that was essential to this volume.

Mary Case assumed the role of ICE facilitator in 2013 and worked with us in rethinking the Institute for Cultural Entrepreneurship and how a case study should unfold. Mark Isaksen, senior museum program officer at the Institute of Museum and Library Services has been our advisor throughout the planning, pilot, and implementation phases of the project and offered sage advice and suggestions. Our editor, Charles Harmon, exhibited infinite patience and understanding for which we are most thankful.

ONE

Centre d'histoire de Montréal

A Museum Finds Its Audience-Focused Niche

Gretchen Sullivan Sorin

In 1983, the City of Montreal converted a turn-of-the-century fire station on Place d'Youville into the Centre d'histoire de Montréal. The renovation of the old horse-drawn and later steam pumper firehouse that closed in 1972 provided an adaptive reuse for a beautiful, architect-designed Queen Anne–style building located in the heart of the oldest neighborhood in Quebec's most populous city. The concept for the new museum "was to create an interpretation centre that would showcase the city's built heritage—its true collection."[1] However, it would take the museum over twenty-five years to find its true purpose in the voices and memories of the people of Montreal.

A TALE OF THREE MUSEUMS

The Quebec Ministry of Cultural Affairs entered into an agreement with the City of Montreal in the 1970s to redevelop the historic "Old City" and to encourage tourism. The agreement led to the establishment of a system of cultural centers, including the Centre d'histoire de Montréal, a US National Park Service–style interpretation center designed primarily as an orientation center for visitors to the city. The new interpretive center housed a permanent chronological exhibition, *Montreal Five Times*, on the first floor. The exhibition featured panels, videos, and a limited number of objects that offered tourists an overview of Montreal history beginning in 1535. Gradually the interpretive center evolved into more of an urban

1

Figure 1.1. Exhibition at Centre d'histoire de Montréal. *Courtesy Centre d'histoire de Montréal.*

museum, adding temporary exhibitions upstairs and serving as the primary repository for a host of artifacts salvaged from around the city. For example, a light post from Expo 67 discovered in the city made its way to the Centre d'histoire.

At the time of its founding, the mission of the Centre d'histoire identified its market primarily as travelers to the city. Montreal's permanent residents were viewed as a secondary audience. With the focus on tourism and little to see except permanent overview exhibitions, the city's residents were unlikely to visit more than once unless they had guests visiting from out of town. The staff viewed the Centre d'histoire de Montréal as the institution in the city that was most focused on telling the story of the broad sweep of Montreal's history from the First Nations settlement to the present.

Between 1983 and 2003, two other museums in the city developed major overview history exhibitions about Montreal and carved niches for themselves as primary sites to tell the city's history. The McCord Museum, a history collecting and research institution affiliated with McGill University, the major English university in the city, created *Montreal — Points of View*, a core Montreal history exhibition. The exhibition "explored 10 different facets of the history of Montreal, from its earliest residents to the city of today with its metro and skyscrapers."[2] In 2013, the museum sought to make the history of the city more relevant to local citizens and encourage repeat visitation by creating changing exhibitions of local contemporary photographers.

The second museum, Pointe à Callière, just two blocks from Centre d'histoire de Montréal, is an important national historical and archaeological site. The site resembles a cloche placed on top of the land that contained part of the oldest white settlement in the city as well as the point where First Nations people camped. This relatively young museum in the old city neighborhood opened in 1992, a legacy gift to the city from the nation.

The new museum in the city provided a very specific, unusual, and engaging type of visitor experience. Visitors descended from the ground level to the lower level below ground and emerged among the archaeological ruins. Tour guides and interpretive exhibitions guided visitors through archaeological dig sites, providing stopping points that depicted aspects of the city at different periods. With the support of video assistance, visitors observed an ancient cemetery burial, visited the site of the original market, and discovered the remnants of Montreal's fetid river that became its first sewer and facilitated the sweep of cholera through the city in 1832. Pointe à Callière provided the best type of archaeological interpretation, enabling visitors to experience the authentic archaeological evidence of Montreal's past. But the experience was static. The archaeological site — the evidence of the city's past — remains frozen in time.

Although primarily an archaeological site, Pointe à Callière introduced its tour experience through a very energetic, three-dimensional, multimedia film that chronologically charted the history of the city from the glacial formation of Quebec to its current configuration. The pro-Montreal film served as a general orientation for tourists to the city.

With the McCord Museum and Pointe à Callière characterizing themselves as the city's history-focused institutions, the Centre d'histoire de Montréal became just one of three history institutions with similar and somewhat competing missions. To differentiate itself, the Centre d'histoire sought to redefine itself and to find its special niche and the most compelling need in the largest city in the province of Quebec. The museum did not want to be just another place that told the story of Montreal but wanted to serve a useful purpose in the city. The museum wanted to matter.

FINDING A NICHE

The fact that the Centre d'histoire de Montréal was a city-owned museum meant that historian and director Jean-François Leclerc constantly had to prove the museum's value and purpose to elected officials to ensure its continued funding. As a municipal museum, the Centre d'histoire's budget depended entirely on the city's largesse. Most importantly, Leclerc had to demonstrate that the museum was not duplicating services but rather was providing something special for the local citizenry that was worthy of ongoing public support. With multiple institutions competing for the opportunity to tell the city's story, Leclerc looked for additional ways to distinguish his small interpretive center so that both city officials and the general public would feel that the museum provided an essential community service.

After years of trying to increase the museum's share of the city's cultural budget, city officials hinted to Leclerc that they might consider increasing his budget if he attracted a larger audience. As a long-standing director in Montreal, Leclerc also knew that such a strategy could backfire if the Centre d'histoire's visitation subsequently dropped and, with it, city funding. Still, broad support across the city through ongoing oral history projects that continually brought new groups and new constituents into the fold meant that the museum could position itself to serve multiple local constituencies and preserve a history that was not being addressed by other institutions.

Director Leclerc's first experiment to establish a niche for the Centre d'histoire was to establish a museum within a museum. A Brazilian model provided the inspiration for this new approach. The Museum of the Person, Latin America's largest oral history project, shares the voices of over ten thousand people with the public through the Internet, virtual reference centers, books, and exhibitions. Established at a time when the Brazilian government told the official state story and ignored the experiences that did not reinforce its version of the past, the Museum of the Person filled in some of these blanks by telling history from the bottom up, and it resonated with a wide audience. This model, as implemented in Montreal's history center, lasted for five years. It was not working well because the city's museum of the person—as a separate institution—competed with the goals of the Centre d'histoire. Restructuring was in order.

Leclerc still wanted to use oral histories as the focus of the museum and use these stories to develop relationships with people throughout the city. He conceptualized an idea that became known as the memory clinic and in 2009 hired Catherine Charlebois to implement the museum's new mission to focus on the oral histories of the citizens of Montreal. In this model, tourists would become the secondary audience. Charlebois, a native of Montreal, worked in the education department of the McCord Museum but had experiences in both collections and education. Her first position in the United States had been as curator of a living history museum with a large and diverse collection. During graduate school at the Cooperstown Graduate Program of Museum Studies, she had gained exhibition experience and an interest in working with history from the ground up. The Cooperstown program was well known for its focus on training students to work closely with communities and to document traditional practices.

Charlebois's hiring was a signal to the entire museum that change was coming; the museum's center of gravity was shifting. Managing oral history projects became a creative way to directly involve local citizens in the museum. It also provided a vehicle to document and support immigrant groups, lower-income communities, and others who were generally not a part of the city's written historical record.[3]

Charlebois's first task was to implement a memory clinic. Borrowing the format of the health-care industry's neighborhood blood clinics, the museum organized a shared and very public opportunity for neighborhood members to "donate" their memories to trained staff. The Centre d'histoire chose Montreal's Portuguese community as its pilot neighborhood. Without written or tangible history, the story of the Portuguese in Montreal remained largely undocumented. The Centre d'histoire's first steps were to develop links with the citizens in the neighborhood and to work with them to gather preliminary information on the Portuguese experience in Montreal. During the memory clinic, the staff, wearing white coats like medical professionals, collected stories on videotape and gathered names as future contacts to conduct longer interviews. They also invited neighborhood residents to bring cherished artifacts to be photographed.

Another memory clinic documented the stories of residents at Habitations Jeanne-Mance, a low-income housing project built in the city in

1957. Within the city, the housing project, like most urban renewal projects, did not have a good reputation. But the memory clinic uncovered a different attitude among residents. To the families who lived at Habitations Jeanne-Mance, the housing project provided an escape from the Montreal slums. Jeanne-Mance housing project staff, at first skeptical of the idea of the memory clinic, soon embraced it when they discovered the potential it held for humanizing the residents in ways that other approaches had not.

On the day of the clinic at Habitations Jeanne-Mance, the museum pitched a large tent in the community, giving the museum maximum visibility and creating almost a festival atmosphere. It was the Centre d'histoire's first outdoor memory clinic and on a technical level posed several challenges, including videotaping with street noise. Still, more than five hundred people participated in the day's festivities. According to Charlebois, the residents found the sessions particularly gratifying. "The first impact was, I have a say. My voice was heard." The stories collected through the memory clinic complemented other scholarly research being done by a Université du Québec à Montréal researcher whose work catalogued the problems of the projects. In contrast, the oral histories offered inside points of view that were personal and visceral. Uncensored, the stories catalogued both positive and negative stories of urban renewal from the people who experienced it. The memory clinic also made the community aware of the Centre d'histoire de Montréal and its value in the city, an ancillary but very important benefit.[4]

Following their memory clinic, the staff at Habitations Jeanne-Mance requested that the Centre d'histoire broaden the project to include a celebration of its fiftieth anniversary. Rather than creating a physical exhibition, they asked that the museum share the stories it collected in a virtual format so that it would be more widely available to all of the residents of Montreal. Like the projects modeled by Brazil's Museum of the Person, the wide dissemination of information about the residents of the housing project contributed greatly to community pride and helped to make all of Montreal's citizens aware of the people who lived at Habitations Jeanne-Mance.

In addition to the "samples" collected through the memory clinics, the museum adopted other new programs that took it deeper into its commitment to focus on oral storytelling. Memory-mapping techniques and experimentation with various individual and group interviews enabled the Centre d'histoire to determine the best methods to gather oral histories from different individuals and groups. Programs like "You're Part of History," aimed at high school students newly arrived in the city, captured family memories of immigration. The most challenging program the museum adopted was the production of exhibitions based on "oral history investigations" that gave voice to all of Montreal's people, including "Montreal's cultural communities, outcast workers, neighborhood histories, and low cost housing living experiences." The first exhibition undertaken in this category, *Lost Neighborhoods*, created a model for visual presentation based on oral history that provided a model for other museums but, most importantly, dramatically increased the museum's visitation to its downtown sites.

MISSION CHANGE: EMBRACING ORAL HISTORY AND PERSONAL MEMORIES

In 2010 the Centre d'histoire de Montréal officially changed its mission statement to embrace this new vision:

> The mission of the Centre d'histoire de Montréal, the city's own history museum, is to transmit a better understanding of the city, its cultural diversity and both its tangible and intangible heritage. Through public engagement, the museum offers its expertise to citizens and seeks to integrate their stories and mementoes into upcoming exhibits and activities. It reveals how Montrealers have forged the urban environment and defined the metropolis' identity.

This vision recognized the change to focus on the local citizens of Montreal and to document their stories through oral histories. *Lost Neighborhoods* became the first exhibition using this new approach. To provide access to the broadest possible audiences, all of the audio components of the exhibition were provided either in English with French translation or French with English translation.

An important collection of photographs that documented the lost neighborhoods provided the basis for this exhibition. In the 1950s, not all of Montreal looked like the modern city that its leaders hoped to present to the world. Major modernization projects that led to the World's Fair (Expo 67) and the 1976 Summer Olympics required new buildings and acres of space. Before tearing down the three blighted neighborhoods to make room for these economic development efforts, the city created a detailed photographic inventory of each building slated for demolition and urban renewal. This collection of images provided a rich source of visual material on the three lost neighborhoods—the red-light district, Faubourg à m'lasse, and Goose Village.

The *Lost Neighborhoods* exhibition used personal testimonies from former residents of these communities plus the memories of the city officials and others involved in the demolition of these neighborhoods and the modernization of the city. Visitors to the museum had the opportunity to draw their own conclusions as they listened to each interviewee tell his or her story and express opinions about the destruction of the neighborhoods, the nature of everyday life, or the push for modernization and the quest to clean up the slums. Attitudes, of course, depended on the teller's point of view.

Centered on what the museum staff referred to as "intangible heritage," the Centre d'histoire pioneered a way of using the oral histories as the primary visual presentation strategy in their exhibitions. Visitors traveling through the exhibition listened to compelling video storytelling set among environments that suggested the physical feeling of the neighborhoods that were lost. One vignette, for example, simulated an abandoned living room replete with broken plaster, trash on the floor, a frayed, overstuffed chair, and a 1950s television. The collected memories were projected on the television screen. At various points in the exhibition, photographs and maps oriented visitors to the sites and provided context. Unlike the orientation history exhibitions, *Lost Neighborhoods* provided a forum for individuals who lived in the city to consider critical issues related to life in Montreal, from the effects of urban renewal to future concerns about planning and development.

At Centre d'histoire de Montréal, *Lost Neighborhoods* also set the stage for other exhibitions based on oral testimony that address topics relevant to modern-day Montrealers. According to Centre d'histoire curator Charlebois, "The special exhibition topics are very carefully chosen. The topics capture the public imagination and enable us to identify community partners."

The new exhibition that opened in November 2013 is called *Scandale! Vice, Crime and Morality in Montreal, 1940–1960*, and it highlights one of the neighborhoods discussed in the *Lost Neighborhoods* exhibition—the red-light district. When Prohibition passed in the United States, Montreal emerged during and after the ban on alcohol as a city of pleasure, gambling, and nightlife. American tourists found all-night bars, restaurants, and nightclubs hosting some of the most popular performers of the day in this vibrant city a few hours from New York City. But Montreal was not just a place of guilty legal pleasures. It also had an underside of brothels, gambling, and organized crime. Corrupt public officials and the murder of a gambling kingpin led to a reform movement in the city. *Scandale!* explores such perpetually current issues as public corruption and the role of vice, religion, and social reform in urban politics.

Scandale! gave the museum the opportunity to identify new community partners and to continue to take its programs and services out into the community. Quartier des Spectacles, Montreal's theater district, is located at the heart of the former red-light district and is the setting for the current exhibition. A consortium of cultural venues in the district—theaters, the symphony, and art galleries—funded a cell-phone walking tour based on the exhibition and the oral history interviews. Ultimately, the collaboration will include a more permanent exhibition inspired by *Scandale!* and developed by the museum to be housed at a site within the theater district.

What's next for the Centre d'histoire de Montréal? The museum anticipates looking at the conflict between agriculture and urban life and encouraging people to think about issues of feeding the people who live in the city. Urban agriculture and where food comes from are issues of current concern and the importance of the farms surrounding the city, the farmers' markets throughout the city, and the foods that are consumed are issues of vital importance to urban residents.

CONCLUSION

After almost a quarter of a century, the Centre d'histoire de Montréal found a niche that made its services desirable and useful to city residents, including those who might not ordinarily be museumgoers. The museum's exhibitions changed from simply introducing tourists to the city and all of its positive attributes to providing a comfortable forum in which local citizens could learn and talk about urban problems and issues that affect their daily lives. In addition, the Centre d'histoire became the place that collected and preserved the memories of those whose history had not traditionally been a valued part of the written record, and as such, they made and continue to make an important contribution to the story of Montreal's past. Preserving memories became a service that community groups did not know they needed but now sought to attain. Charlebois noted, "The museum offers its expertise to cultural communities, companies, boroughs, and neighborhoods in their memory-gathering initiatives and commemoration events." Its mission is to bring the public to discover and appreciate the valuable memories rooted in the territory, heritage, and history of Montreal. Charlebois continued, "We think of ourselves as 'a small giant.' We are not the largest museum. We don't have the same means as other institutions, but we do things in the best way."

NOTES

1. Centre d'histoire de Montréal, http://ville.montreal.qc.ca/portal/page?_pageid= 9077,102021580&_dad=portal&_schema=PORTAL, accessed December 28, 2013.
2. The McCord Museum, http://www.mccord-museum.qc.ca/expositions/expositionsXSL.php?lang=1&expoId=71&page=accueil, accessed November 10, 2013.
3. Interview with Catherine Charlebois, October 31, 2013.
4. Interview with Catherine Charlebois, October 31, 2013.

TWO

The Weeksville Heritage Center

Pamela Green

Weeksville, located in what is now the Crown Heights neighborhood of Brooklyn, New York, was founded in 1838 by free African American James Weeks. The community, populated by freemen and freed slaves, was the first independent free black community in the country. By the 1850s, Weeksville was a thriving community of five hundred people and included homes with gardens, businesses, a school, church, hospital, orphanage, and newspaper. By 1950, Weeksville had vanished.

The Weeksville Heritage Center details the forty-year journey of rediscovery, preservation, and expansion of Weeksville as a historic site. Hampered by a difficult location and subject to a number of environmental shocks, the Weeksville Heritage Center found success through extending the definition of community that defined Weeksville to the current-day community surrounding the historic site. By engaging the local community, the Weeksville Heritage Center has built relevancy and sustainability.

INTRODUCTION

Weeksville Heritage Center, established in 1968 and chartered in 1971 by the New York State Education Department, is both a historic preservation organization and a community cultural center located in the Crown Heights neighborhood of central Brooklyn, New York. At the heart of the center are the historic Hunterfly Road Houses, three nineteenth-century wood-frame structures that were homes to early African American residents of the community of Weeksville and predate the Civil War and the

Figure 2.1.   Joan Maynard and Students, ca. 1985, Weeksville Heritage Center.
Courtesy Weeksville Heritage Center

nationwide abolition of slavery. The Society for the Preservation of
Weeksville and Bedford Stuyvesant History is steward to the Historic
Hunterfly Road Houses.

Weeksville is unique in that African American entrepreneurs and land
investors intentionally organized the community to promote economic,
social, and political rights for African Americans as full American citizens. Weeksville residents were activists who created and sustained a
number of important African American institutions, including churches,
one of the first fully integrated schools, an orphanage, a home for the
elderly, two newspapers, and antislavery organizations. Many prominent
residents, journalists, clergy, laborers, educators, and, most importantly,
everyday people resided in the community. They advocated for abolition
and provided safe haven for freedom seekers escaping slavery in other
parts of the country and for exiles fleeing Manhattan during the violent
draft riots of the Civil War era in New York City in 1863.

The three historic houses are surrounded by an enormous green space
that comprises almost an entire city block and is located within two of the
largest communities of black residents in New York City, Crown Heights
and nearby Bedford-Stuyvesant. Weeksville is also located directly across
the street from the Kingsborough Houses, one of the largest housing
projects in New York City. In 1990, 36 percent of residents of the Crown
Heights neighborhood were living below the poverty line.[1] In the early
days of Weeksville's preservation, the society was often asked to consider
moving the houses to a "safer and more convenient" location.

FINDING AND PRESERVING WEEKSVILLE: 1967–2001

In 1967, the little-known community of Weeksville was the subject of study by a community group taking an adult extension course with Pratt Institute professor James Hurley. Hurley, along with one of the students, a pilot, Joseph Haynes, obtained a plane and flew over the Crown Heights neighborhood. While in the air, Hurley noticed four houses that were facing off the city grid. Research showed that the houses, built in the 1840s, 1850s, 1865, and 1883, were facing Hunterfly Road, an old Dutch and Indian trading road. Weeksville had been found.

In 1969, artist and activist Joan Maynard, a member of the study group, organized the Society for the Preservation of Weeksville and Bedford Stuyvesant History. Hurley arranged for the first archaeological dig of the newly discovered site in a successful attempt to save the houses from being demolished as part of the city's urban renewal project. Photographs, clothing, ceramics, and other items were found, confirming the presence of the past Weeksville community.

During the 1970s, Maynard worked to secure the historic site by garnering community support among residents, schoolchildren, and others. Schoolchildren from the Weeksville school also raised one thousand dollars to support Weeksville. Supporters, including schoolchildren, rode in a yellow school bus to the Landmarks Preservation Commission to ask for New York City landmark status. The Hunterfly Houses were designated as a New York City landmark in 1970, and in 1971, the society was chartered by the New York State Department of Education. In 1972, the Hunterfly Houses were listed in the National Register of Historic Places and Joan Maynard became president of the society.[2] The houses were purchased by the society in 1973 and 1974.[3] In 1977, using funds from foundations and matching grants, restoration of the four homes began.

By the 1980s, the partially rehabilitated homes were open for tours. Residents of the Kingsborough Houses used the Weeksville space for community gardens. The Weeksville Family Day was created as a way to say thanks to the community for keeping alive the legacy of the nineteenth-century settlement. By 1983, two of the four houses were completed; however, additional funding was needed to complete the other houses.

The 1990s proved to be a difficult decade for Weeksville. In December 1990, vandals ripped out plaster walls, sinks, and cabinets and removed plumbing in the houses in a search for copper pipes. The heating system failed, and the resulting water damage destroyed much of the restoration work.[4] In 1993, the 1865 house caught fire and had to be completely rebuilt, and in 1996, a car crashed into one of the houses, causing more damage and the need for additional funds for repairs.[5] Even with these difficulties, the Weeksville Society, under Maynard's leadership, had become an anchor in central Brooklyn, a leader in preserving the early history of African Americans in Brooklyn and one of the first grassroots preservation organizations in the country.

In 1999, Maynard retired after nearly thirty years at the helm. Several foundations and individuals came together to create a transition oversight committee. The committee engaged in extensive institutional and capital planning and conducted two executive director searches, resulting in the hiring of Pam Green as the new executive director.

Green was not a traditional candidate for the position of executive director of a historical society. She had no experience in the field of history, museums, or historic sites. Her background included working as a computer programmer, commercial banking executive, consultant to minority businesses and nonprofit organizations, executive director of a food bank, food and hunger policy coordinator for the City of New York, assistant commissioner for the Agency for Child Development for New York City, and vice president for strategic partners at Sesame Workshop. The board hired her and charged her with achieving three goals: restore the houses and historic site, fund and build a major expansion, and create the infrastructure to support the expansions and future goals of the society.

INITIAL DECISIONS AND CHANGE: 2001–2005

As Green began work on September 4, 2001, she considered her options. She knew there was much work to be accomplished. In 2001, the Weeksville Society was slowly coming back from the edge of closing. The mission of the organization at that time was to collect, preserve, research, interpret, educate, and disseminate knowledge and information about historic Weeksville and the African American experience in Central Brooklyn from the nineteenth century to the present. As of 2001, the mission statement was realized through irregularly scheduled tours and the Weeksville Family Day Festival. On average, seven thousand visitors came to Weeksville annually, largely through school tours and the festival. Like most small community-based organizations, the society's funding came primarily from New York City agencies, small foundation and corporate grants, and a few individual donors. Funding and staffing varied from year to year.

Although working with a limited budget of $500,000 and a small staff (an administrator, financial director, and caretaker), Green was optimistic. While there was no formal vision statement, the organization's focus was to make its collections, programs, and services more accessible through the restored historic houses and site and through a new museum. A new board president was in place, board reorganization was beginning, public and private funding were in place to begin the restoration of the historic Hunterfly Road Houses, and there was initial funding to build an African American museum on the Weeksville grounds.

One week into Green's tenure as executive director, the Twin Towers collapsed during the 9/11 attack on New York City. In the aftermath, the demands on funders and how funders viewed their roles drastically changed. The mayor of New York City and the governor of New York State collectively cut billions from the budget.[6] Many funders redirected resources to meet the needs of service organizations. Funders who were still providing grants to cultural organizations were either not funding historical societies or had adopted stringent requirements for demonstrated sustainability. Despite the progress the society had made in stabilizing the organization and developing realistic planning documents, Weeksville did not yet have sufficient documentation to position itself as a sustainable cultural organization. Weeksville fell to the bottom of the list of organizations considered for funding. Green worried that the lack of consistent, ongoing funding would destabilize the society and threaten the work that had been done. She realized that if the organization was going to be able to convince funders of its importance to its community and to children and families, there needed to be an extraordinary increase in visibility, awareness, impact, and relevance.

Green also faced a number of challenges in meeting the goals set by the board. New York City and private resources had committed significant capital funding to restore the historic site. Green knew that the capital funding couldn't be turned down or safely deferred. The restoration of the houses had to continue even without adequate staffing or a revised infrastructure. Yet the houses would have to be closed for an extended period of time to complete the restoration, making it difficult for the center to offer essential programming. In addition, in order to stabilize and grow funding, Green needed to find ways for the organization to demonstrate its viability and support from others, something that would be made more difficult by the closing of the historic houses.

Green also inherited a strong founder culture. Retired founder and former executive director Joan Maynard had led the organization for over thirty years. Staff were loyal to Maynard, the community and traditional funders equated Weeksville with Maynard, and standards and expectations were based on Maynard's leadership. Maynard's passion and drive had secured and preserved Weeksville, but Green knew that changes were needed to complete the expansion and move the organization forward. In short, Green had to find a way to secure funding, build staff, develop the board, offer programming without access to the houses, move forward with the house restoration and expansion plans, and change the culture of the organization, all with limited staff resources and uncertain funding.

Funding

Over the next two years, Green sought to stabilize the organization financially by working to eliminate accounts payable and responding to funder requirements. In addition, after 9/11, when it became clear that funding from traditional sources would be hard to obtain, the board and staff decided to hold a gala fund-raising event.[7] The first-time gala grossed over $159,000 and netted nearly $100,000. The gala became an annual affair which accounted for nearly one third of the organization's operating revenue. In subsequent years, the gala moved to Manhattan to attract a broader corporate audience and potential honoree pool. At its height, the gala grossed more than $550,000 and always netted at least 50 percent of the gross receipts.

During 2002 and 2003, the society was able to obtain funding by collaborating with the Brooklyn Public Library to begin intensive research into the Weeksville history, something that had been lacking. Historical findings would help the society achieve national significance on the National Register of Historic Places, and accurate information was needed to innovatively interpret the historic houses and create engaging tours and other programming. Scholarly research also instantly added to the credibility of the organization. The collaboration led to creation of a traveling exhibit, seminars, changes to the annual festival, and an enhanced ability to obtain small grants from new sources.

Staffing

Green wanted to bring a new level of professionalism and higher level of creativity to the organization, but funding for staffing was severely limited. Before hiring additional staff, Green wanted to determine what positions were absolutely essential to move the organization forward and what financial resources were available to cover the salaries and begin offering benefits to staff. Her goal was to create an efficient but lean organization with highly skilled professionals who were able to take on multiple tasks in the short term. Given the organization's financial limitations, a conscious decision was made to work with the original staff. To fill staffing gaps, two part-time staff were hired: a director of education and program development and, to address the lack of consistent funding, a development director who had extensive experience in fund-raising for cultural institutions. Her connections to people in foundations and corporations enabled her to quickly set up meetings for Green and the director of education and program development and to favorably position the society for future funding. Within three to four years, the society's revenue streams were completely diversified and its reputation among funders strengthened. Green's familiarity with funders from her days at the food bank also proved invaluable in stabilizing the society's finances.

Board Development

Green also had to tackle the redevelopment of the board. Traditionally, the society's board was made up of community members. By 2001, at least two corporate representatives had been brought onto the board, but more diversity was needed. Over the next three years, at least ten new board members were recruited, including representatives from corporate, philanthropic, health, financial, and academic areas. New board policies were established, including a give/get policy and an amendment of the bylaws.

Programming during the Restoration

One of Green's biggest challenges was to offer programming and maintain visibility in the community while the houses were being restored. Staff and the nine-hundred-item collection needed to be moved to alternative sites, and the society did not have funding to pay for storage. Green found a rent-free location for staff operations and negotiated storage space in one of the high schools in downtown Brooklyn, which also offered a beneficial programming collaboration. The society began working in and with the senior citizens' residence across the street and collaborated with other cultural organizations, including a group promoting tourism in Brooklyn.

Culture Change

Green used changes in procedures to begin changing the organizational culture at Weeksville. She established formal hours for tours, created ongoing programs, and reached outside of the traditional funding sources to request funding for programs. Cataloguing and archiving papers and artifacts was deferred until funding was available to do the job correctly. (Ultimately, this meant that collections would not be displayed until the houses were restored.) The Family Day Festival was reorganized. Free food (too costly) and activities that did not relate to Weeksville were eliminated while history-based and substantive activities were added. In 2005, the organization changed its mission statement, name (from Weeksville Society to the Weeksville Heritage Center), and logo, and created a vision statement.

Of all of the changes, the decision to change the logo was the most contentious. For more than thirty years, a tintype of a well-dressed woman, dubbed the Weeksville Lady and found during one of the archaeological digs, was used as the symbol of Weeksville. However, no proof existed that the woman on the tintype lived at Weeksville. The new logo, which featured the outline of a house and a road encircled by the name Weeksville Heritage Society, supported the new vision statement:

Weeksville Heritage Center is a premiere cultural institution offering innovative, socially conscious learning experiences in history, art, environment and technology. We are a catalyst for change based on the legacy of the historic Weeksville residents who created a thriving community modeling entrepreneurship, self-sufficiency and creativity. We use the historic site, the physical landscape and programming to highlight the creativity, entrepreneurship and self-sufficiency demonstrated by historic Weeksville's residents.

FINDING RELEVANCY AND SUSTAINABILITY: 2005–2009

In 2005, after nearly forty years of raising funds to fully protect and restore the houses, all three houses were opened to the public for the first time. Implementation of a historic furnishing plan and restoring the houses to three different eras, 1860s, 1900s, and 1930s, provided insight into how life in Weeksville changed over time. The restoration of the interior and exterior of the houses and the grounds, which were appropriately landscaped to complement the houses, garnered awards. Historic Weeksville came alive through tours based on extensive research, the display of items found at the site, exciting public programming, an oral history project, symposia, presentations, and school literacy, arts education, and media arts programming.

To drive visitorship, staff began to consider new programming for the restored site. For the first time, tour scripts were based on the research and a walking tour was created. A preservation education program was developed to introduce high school students to carpentry and other preservation skills. When the program became too expensive to maintain, it was redesigned. The new preservation education program involved working with students, in school, to teach them about the cultural assets in their community. Students developed innovative ways of disseminating this information, including creating iPod tours and an exhibition.

Agricultural self-sufficiency was an important part of the historical Weeksville community, where residents once grew and preserved their own fruits and vegetables. Ironically, Central Brooklyn, including the current-day neighborhood of Crown Heights, had become a food desert, defined by the 2008 Farm Bill as an "area in the United States with limited access to affordable and nutritious food, particularly such an area composed of predominantly lower-income neighborhoods and communities."[8] Most of the neighborhood food stores were bodegas, small neighborhood stores which carried a narrower range of products at higher prices than supermarkets. Few bodegas carried fresh fruits and vegetables. Not surprisingly, a 2006 report by the New York City Department of Health found higher rates of obesity among adults living in nearby Bedford-Stuyvesant, and a 2003 study found that 20 percent of Central

Brooklyn residents identified themselves as in "poor" or "fair" health, compared to 14 percent nationwide.[9]

In response, the Green Weeksville Program introduced elementary students to Weeksville's agricultural history by providing opportunities for the students to plant and grow fresh produce in the gardens created during the restoration. Green Weeksville provided a forum for students and the community to make connections between traditional gardening, health, nutrition, and current environmental issues. The produce grown in the gardens was supplemented by produce from upstate New York farmers supporting the establishment of the society's farmer's market in 2005.[10] The highly successful market offered affordable, easily obtainable fresh fruits and vegetables to the surrounding community.

The July Salon Series was created to introduce the community to emerging artists and as a way of bringing new audiences to Weeksville. Initially, live musical performances were held every Saturday in July and featured musicians who were more traditional in nature. Staff experimented with several formats, including requiring musicians to talk about the history of their music as a tie-in to Weeksville and developing a theme for each year's series. Eventually, the July Salon Series became an afternoon/early evening of relaxing music for families and adults by artists seldom accessible for the suggested donation of about five dollars. Additional society programs included symposia and speakers' panels dealing with topics as current as gentrification and as historical as black journalism in the nineteenth century. Workshops throughout the year covered areas from eco-friendly cleaning products to creating thaumatropes, a popular nineteenth-century toy.

In addition to creating relevant programming, the society broke ground on a 19,000-square-foot new museum in 2009. Green and her staff realized that the definition of the museum had to change. The traditional image of an African American museum was not going to be relevant to Weeksville history or to the surrounding community. Although stakeholders had been brought together to discuss the vision, there had been little, if any, real thought or encouragement given to thinking outside of the box. Staff began to call the new building an education and cultural arts facility. The vision that emerged was to have a place which brought all the staff together; provided the opportunity to expand educational and public programming through year-round public performances; offered space for local and traveling exhibits, retail, and food; and was engaging enough in design and activities to be open most of the days of the week.

At the heart of the vision was a commitment to provide a contemporary experience to the visitor based on the historic stories of Weeksville and recognition that innovative and engaging activities were needed to garner return visits. In keeping with the newest mission statement, "to document, preserve and interpret the history of free African American communities in Weeksville, Brooklyn and beyond and to create and inspire innovative, contemporary uses of African American history through education, the arts, and civic engagement," Green and her staff envisioned a fun-filled active and interactive space which contextualized the story of Weeksville, past, present, and future, through an orientation exhibition and ongoing workshops about ecology, technology, literacy, and media arts.

CONCLUSION

In reflecting on the changes put in place to accomplish the goals laid out by the board of directors, Green described the process as "totally organic" with little formal planning. Because funding was neither consistent nor guaranteed for operations and staff resources were limited, the society was not able to follow a comprehensive strategic or business plan for developing an organization and building infrastructure. In the short run, research suffered, as did capacity building, marketing, and archival efforts. The society focused on its physical assets, restoring the houses, and working with volunteers to protect the site while working on the design of the new building.

Success was defined in a variety of ways: being able to engage people with new experimental programming, completion of and outlets for the traveling exhibit, or new funder involvement with Weeksville. According to Green, "When funders and neighbors could begin to see how our site could help empower the community by giving them tools through an education in history to face the challenges of their time, then staff knew it might be on the right path and that was considered success."

While location continues to present challenges for the organization, Green notes that it was important for the society to help people realize that the site's location as a cultural oasis in the middle of the inner city makes it unique:

> Ultimately, Weeksville Heritage Center will serve as a resource for all present day New Yorkers by sharing the special story of the early Weeksville pioneers who survived against great odds. Like our neighbors, the residents of Kingsborough Housing Project continue to pursue their dreams of controlling their destiny under odds arguably just as challenging. The restoration process itself, with its peaks of progress and valleys of setbacks, represents the general situation of our home community here in the inner city. The successful completion of the preservation project and its expansion symbolize for many the use of historic preservation as a powerful tool.

As Joan Maynard said, "It is essential that places like Weeksville, where the human spirit survived and succeeded, be preserved for future generations to see, touch, and celebrate."[11]

NOTES

1. Crown Heights neighborhood map, accessed November 10, 2013, http://www.city-data.com/neighborhood/Crown-Heights-Brooklyn-NY.html.

2. Nichole M. Christian, "Hidden in Brooklyn, a Bit of Black History; Freedmen's Homes Seen as Attraction," *New York Times*, October 29, 2001, sec. F.

3. "Weeksville Buys Historic Houses: Sees Cost of $200,000," *New York Times*, June 24, 1973, p. 93.

4. Arnold Berke, "Vandals Attack Brooklyn's Weeksville," *Preservation News*, March 1, 1991, p. 9, accessed November 24, 2013, http://prn.library.cornell.edu/cgi-bin/cornell-prn?a=d&d=PRN19910301.2.22&e=-------en-20--1--txt-IN------#.

5. Charisse Jones, "Unearthing the Tales of a Lost Settlement: Glimpses of Black History," *New York Times*, April 22, 1996.

6. Christian, "Hidden in Brooklyn."

7. Pam Green, phone interview with Lynne Sessions, November 13, 2013.

8. "USDA Food Desert Locator Tool—Frequently Asked Questions," accessed November 10, 2013, http://apps.ams.usda.gov/fooddeserts/FAQLocatorTool2-pgr.pdf.

9. Just Food Farm School NYC, Apprenticeship Site—Weeksville Heritage Center, accessed November 9, 2013, http://www.justfood.org/farm-school-nyc/apprenticeship-site-weeksville-heritage-center.

10. *Con Edison Immigrant Artist Program Newsletter*, no. 30, NYFA, accessed July 28, 2014, http://current.nyfa.org/post69197768418/iap-newsletter-issue-30.

11. Pam Green, "Civic Engagement on a Shoestring: The Weeksville Society Experience," presentation at National Park Service's "Great Places Great Debates: Opening Historic Sites to Civic Engagement" conference, New York, NY, April 1–2, 2004.

THREE

Becoming the Capital Region's Living Room

Philip Morris and Proctors Theatre

Nicholas DeMarco

A 1920s vaudeville house built by Frederick Francis Proctor in Schenecta-dy, New York, successfully transitions to film, changes hands, and falls into disrepair in the 1970s. The theater is seized by the city of Schenecta-dy for back taxes, saved by a community group, and ultimately becomes an economic powerhouse, transforming the city and the region. The story of the Proctors transformation is the story of how entrepreneurial vision-ary Philip Morris and a proactive board turned a local not-for-profit arts and culture institution into a driving force for regional economic and community redevelopment and revitalization.

INTRODUCTION

Frederick Francis Proctor, known as the "Dean of Vaudeville Managers," began his career as a theater manager by leasing The Gayety, a small theater on Green Street in Albany, New York. As manager, he imple-mented several innovative ideas: arranging orchestral accompaniments to his shows, improving dressing rooms, and offering employees benefits such as profit sharing and insurance. Improved quality and service in-creased theater attendance.[1] Proctor, who was always on the lookout for new opportunities, noticed how the population of Schenectady, New York, had increased as a result of the presence of two large businesses,

Figure 3.1. View from the Upper Balcony, Proctors Theatre. *Photography by John D. Woolf*

General Electric and American Locomotive Company. Working with architect Thomas Lamb, Proctor designed a grand theater, beginning construction in 1925 and opening in Schenectady on December 27, 1926 to seven thousand paying patrons.[2] The theater featured many vaudeville acts, often pairing five acts with a feature film. As interest in vaudeville waned, the theater's focus on feature films increased. Movie producers perfected sound in the 1930s, and along with performance acts such as comedians and musicians, film became the main attraction.[3]

Proctor passed away in 1929 and most of his fifty theaters were sold to RKO.[4] During the 1950s and '60s, Proctors was mainly a theater house, but by the 1970s the theater had fallen into disrepair and was seized by the city of Schenectady for back taxes. The fate of the theater was bleak; many arts groups and individuals were worried that Proctors would be closed or, worse, demolished. During the summer of 1977, supporters created the Arts Center and Theater of Schenectady Inc. (ACTS) to save Proctors Theatre. The newly formed ACTS board met on May 24, 1978, and voted to accept the deed of the theater with the understanding that the city would perform $100,000 worth of repairs to the roof and heating system.[5] A feasibility study showed that the theater could be an asset to the community. ACTS raised $7,000 and received access to $500,000 of city and federal funds to restore the building. The doors of the newly restored theater opened on January 3, 1979. Magician Harry Blackstone, son of the vaudevillian star who appeared on the same stage many decades before, performed to a standing-room-only audience.[6] The Proctors rebirth had begun.

REBIRTH

The years following the reopening of Proctors were characterized by constant internal change as the organization struggled to balance expansion, programming, and debt. It would take four executive directors, two boards of directors, and thirteen years for the organization to be poised to embrace entrepreneurial innovation in the form of executive director Philip Morris.

The early years at Proctors were filled with an array of programming, and the theater soon became a source of community pride.[7] In 1979, Proctors hired its first professional staff and first executive director, Dennis Madden. Under Madden, the theater expanded programming by bringing in nationally known acts, including Red Skelton, George Carlin, and Bill Cosby. Within five years, Proctors became the largest theater in New York State outside of New York City.[8] The operating budget increased from $100,000 in 1979 to over $2 million by 1984. However, expanded programming came with a cost. In addition to debt from bank loans, losses occurred from overbooking more runs of a show than the community was able to support.[9] By the end of the 1980s, Proctors had accumulated over $1 million in debt. The board demanded something be done to reduce the operating budget. Madden cut $140,000 from the budget by cutting advertising and equipment rental costs and temporarily laying off twenty-two of forty-two employees, most of whom came from box office, custodial, and marketing staff.[10]

In addition to reducing operating costs, Madden planned the "Million Dollar Marathon," a major fund-raising campaign. Local high school students were enlisted to solicit pledges door to door in the hopes they could attend the "Ultimate Party," an all-night event to be held at the city center.[11] The expensive entertainment hired for the event did not appeal to younger audiences, and the fund-raising campaign lost $15,000.[12] The board accepted Madden's offer of resignation in July 1988.

Betty Apkarian, board member and chair of the "Million-Dollar Marathon," enlisted the help of her husband, Harry Apkarian, a local, well-known entrepreneur.[13] As head of a steering committee made up of many of the top business leaders in the area, including Lewis Golub of Price Chopper and William Dake of Stewart's Shops, Apkarian was charged with finding a way to make Proctors financially solvent. One month after Madden resigned, the steering committee presented its findings to the board of trustees.[14] Recommendations included changes in fund-raising, increases in ticket prices, and reductions in the number of production companies. In October, the board met at board president Ernest Kahn's home to consider the steering committee's report and after reviewing the recommendations for reorganization, fired itself.

The original board was made up of community members who were enthusiastic and supportive of the theater but tended to focus on day-today operations. When business leaders joined the board, the board's lack of strategic focus and financial acumen often led them to resign.[15] The new board (largely made up of members from the steering committee) focused on the steering committee's financial plan. The board also appointed a new executive director, Don Schein, the retired president of WMHT, an upstate New York public broadcast organization.[16] Schein agreed to serve without pay until a new executive director was appointed.[17] He brought Gloria Lamere and Fred Daniels to Proctors, both of whom had worked with Schein at WMHT.[18]

Schein realized the importance of booking the right shows at the right volume.[19] He focused on diversifying programming (much of which was recommended by Madden before his departure) and fund-raising. By the end of the 1988–1989 season, there was a projected surplus of $150,000, although with $500,000 owed to local banks, debt was still a major issue.[20] A successful telethon led by Gloria Lamere, who previously led WMHT's televised auction fund-raiser, brought in $750,000, much of which was used for debt reduction.[21] By the end of May, the surplus increased to $220,000, just as Schein stepped down from his position due to health issues. Lamere became managing director and then, in 1990, executive director.[22]

Proctors thrived under Lamere's leadership.[23] Many Broadway shows were sold out, and Lamere drastically lowered institutional debt. Building repairs to the roof, exterior brickwork, and interior of the theater and the restoration of the original stage flooring were paid for with a $315,000 matching grant. By the beginning of the twenty-first century, Proctors had a net worth of $4 million.[24]

As Lamere led theater operations, the board focused on broader policy and long-term planning. In particular, new Broadway shows were growing in size and becoming more expensive to stage. Lamere and the board realized that the Proctors stage would need to be expanded to accommodate the larger shows.

Proctors was not the only theater in the Capital Region grappling with the idea of stage expansion. The Palace Theatre in Albany was smaller in size, offered similar programming, and was also considering an expansion. A local newspaper leaked a story that discussed a potential merger between Proctors and the Palace. The two institutions came together to discuss potential expansion and mergers and conducted a feasibility study to see if there was enough public interest in the expansion of one or both theaters.[25] Three important findings emerged: the region would support a larger, Broadway-presenting theater, two expanded theaters could not be supported, and the stage that enlarged first would be the more dominant of the two theaters.

As talks were being conducted, Lamere became gravely ill, leaving Fred Daniels to handle much of the operation. Lamere passed away in 2001, and Daniels became the acting executive director while the board began a national search for a new executive director.[26] The search committee was looking for an executive director who could lead Proctors, book Broadway shows, and seek innovative solutions to bring Proctors to "the next level."[27] The board president, Apkarian, wanted someone who could lead downtown development.[28] In short, Proctors needed someone who was a leader and a visionary.

The search yielded three candidates, including Philip Morris, executive director of the Arts Council of Chautauqua County in western New York. As executive director of the Arts Council, Morris presided over the renovation of the twelve-hundred-seat Reg Lenna Civic Center in Jamestown, earning the "Best Renovation of a Historic Theatre" award from the League of American Theatres; developed the Lucille Ball Festival of New Comedy; supervised the opening of the Lucille Ball-Desi Arnaz Museum; produced a development corporation that managed urban planning projects; and developed the Arts in Education project that created an artist residency program serving twenty-five schools. While visiting Schenectady, Morris was stunned by how empty the city was but saw great potential for community development. After interviewing Morris, the selection committee recommended him to the board, citing his track record, vision, optimism, and willingness to tackle the issues facing the theater and the community.[29] Morris was offered the executive director's position and began work in March 2002. The board identified four priority issues: implement the stage expansion project, upgrade technology, address staffing issues, and explore new opportunities.

EXPANSION

With Philip Morris at the helm, Proctors turned its attention to the most important priority set by the board, the stage expansion. By this time, talks between Proctors and the Palace had resulted in an agreement that the Palace would expand its stage while Proctors would manage the new Palace facility. Neither side pursued the agreement, so Proctors decided to expand its stage. Morris began working on the expansion project with the Schenectady Metroplex Development Authority. The Metroplex, which was funded through sales tax revenue, was charged with enhancing "the long-term economic vitality of life in Schenectady County" and worked on the revitalization of downtown Schenectady by planning, financing, constructing, administering, and maintaining facilities.[30] Consultants handled feasibility studies for staffing plans and fund-raising.[31]

The feasibility report showed that a change in governance would benefit expansion fund-raising efforts. In 2003, Apkarian, who had served as board president since the board reorganization in the 1980s, stepped down, and Richard Carlstrom agreed to preside over the board for one term.[32] Carlstrom's leadership brought a new style of governance. He did not want to be the face of Proctors; that was Morris's job. Instead, Carl-strom sought to create a higher-functioning board by bringing in new board members who possessed skills needed both for the board and for fund-raising while allowing older members who weren't as active to leave the board. The board evolved into a working board and began to raise funds for the expansion.[33]

With support from the new board, Morris worked closely with both the architect and Director of Facilities Dan Sheehan to plan the expansion. Morris and Sheehan discussed all project details and involved many people in the design process. For example, the stage sat at a low grade, making it difficult to design an easily accessible loading dock. The architect designed long ramps, piers, and lifts to allow road crews to unload the trucks, all at great expense to Proctors. When shows came in during the planning phase of construction, Morris bought pizza for the road crews and asked for input on the loading dock design. The road crews advised Proctors to make the dock a wide space and buy a forklift. Proctors followed the road crews' advice and created a less expensive dock that was easily accessible to traveling productions.[34]

By the end of 2003, Proctors settled on a plan for the $22 million expansion project that called for expanding the stage and renovating the box office, arcade, coffee shop, and retail shops. The nearby Carl Company Building, which had undergone foreclosure in 2002, was purchased in 2004 with a $350,000 grant from Metroplex.[35] The building would house administrative offices and a new I-Werks theater sponsored by General Electric.[36] As plans for Proctors unfolded, Morris introduced a new element to the mix, one he was familiar with during his time in Jamestown: creation of a district plant that would provide cooling and heating to the theater and to the community.

The expanded theater required a new heating and cooling system. The district plant used boilers and chillers to generate and store hot and cold water. The highly efficient system used a continuous loop of hot and cold water to transfer heat and cooling to individually climate-controlled rooms. Exhaust from the plant powered microturbines that cogenerated electricity used by the theater. Powered by natural gas, the plant saved money on utilities while lowering the theater's carbon footprint by forty-six pounds per hour.

The plant had additional benefits. Morris recognized that downtown Schenectady would be in need of utility service as redevelopment began. The system, which could power over a million cubic square feet of downtown property, could be extended to neighboring buildings, allowing Proctors to sell cooling and heating at a discounted rate.[37] Electricity generated by the plant could be purchased as well. Customers would save money while lowering their carbon footprints.[38] Morris received money from the New York State Energy and Research Development Authority (NYSERDA) for a feasibility study. The study identified eight to nine potential customers. After reviewing an economic analysis, the board agreed to create a plant that could serve both Proctors and the immediate community.

As production plans were finalized, the silent phase of the capital campaign moved forward. Metroplex gave Proctors $10 million for the expansion, and Proctors began to raise the rest. Morris pursued $8 million worth of historic tax credits in 2005, but the federal government turned down the initial application because the demolition eliminated too much of the historic material. Undaunted, Morris worked with then-senator Hillary Clinton to appeal the decision and was able to overturn the ruling.[39] The tax credits were modeled after low-income housing tax credits and allowed private-sector businesses with federal tax liabilities and a Department of the Interior–qualified building project to receive a reduction in taxes equal to 25 percent of qualified rehabilitation expenses. In order to take advantage of these credits, Proctors needed to sell them by December 1, 2005, a period of just six weeks. Proctors created a for-profit entity, which in turn would partner with another for-profit business.[40] Proctors received $10 million in credits and quickly entered into a partnership with Sherwin-Williams. Under the IRS K1 process, Proctors sold the credits to Sherwin-Williams. In turn, Sherwin-Williams made a commitment to invest 85 percent of every dollar into the expansion project. Both Proctors and Sherwin-Williams benefited from the partnership. Sherwin-Williams received $10 million worth of historic credits, Proctors received $8.5 million from Sherwin-Williams, and Sherwin-Williams received $1.5 million in tax relief.[41]

Morris also found ways to decrease the cost of the plant through a combination of NYSERDA green energy credits and historic, new market, and New York State Empire Zone property tax credits. He was also able to procure various elements of the plant itself at discounted rates, eliminating some of the plant cost. Within three months of construction of the district plant, the Hampton Inn became Proctors's first energy customer and an immediate revenue source.

In addition to selling heating and cooling, the district plant was used to generate revenue through powering a sidewalk melt system. The city of Schenectady was replacing the sidewalks around Proctors, and the construction gave Proctors the opportunity to install the sidewalk melt system under the sidewalks by its building and throughout the immediate area. The system, which was powered by the heat businesses purchased from Proctors, made the sidewalks safer and lowered insurance costs to Proctors.[42] The money saved on liability insurance was greater than the cost of operating the system.[43]

The construction project broke ground in 2005. Much of the work was paid for with the historic tax credits, local government donations, federal and state grants, and private gifts.[44] Proctors reopened its doors for the 2007–2008 season on September 20, 2007, with a newly expanded stage, enhanced facilities, and a revised name. Marketing and image analysis conducted at the time of the feasibility studies revealed that many people associated the Proctors name with entertainment in the Capital Region. The consultants recommended that Proctors consider this regional appeal when rebranding the theater. The recommendation led to a change in the Proctors name. The apostrophe was dropped, and Proctor's became simply Proctors.[45]

RESTRUCTURING

While construction on the stage expansion was taking place, Morris tackled the other priorities given to him by the board: technology, staffing, and new opportunity exploration. One of the first things Morris noticed was the poor state of technology at Proctors. At the time of his arrival, Proctors only had one e-mail account on one computer that ran on an analog modem. Morris invited the technology specialist he worked with in Jamestown to join him at Proctors, on a part-time basis, to improve technology and communications with one another and with the public.[46] (Ultimately, Proctors was able to provide upgraded technological service to all tenants in its building at a discounted rate.)[47] In particular, Morris implemented Theater Manager, an arts system management software package that provided better information and greater ticketing power and allowed Proctors to track where people found out about a show and evaluate why they bought tickets.[48]

Organizational structure and staffing patterns also needed to be addressed. Morris retained most of the staff. However, lack of technology to support effective communication among staff meant that eight to nine people reported directly to Morris. To improve communication, Morris created four divisions with clearly defined responsibilities: Relationships (fund-raising), headed by Dan Hanifin; Operations, headed by Dan Sheehan; Finance, headed by Kathleen Cetnar; and Programming, headed by Morris himself.[49] Morris presented the new structure to the board in 2007 and suggested that the board restructure committees around the divisions.[50]

Carlstrom, president of the board, agreed and organized the board into a parallel structure. The nominating committee became the governance committee. The governance committee continued to select new board members; however, individuals were now selected based on their skills and connections.[51] The rest of the board was organized into work committees that echoed Morris's divisional structure.[52] A board member was appointed to head each committee, and the senior director of each department met with the committee to discuss policies and issues that affected the area of Proctors covered by the department director. Board meetings were streamlined and provided an open forum for board members to ask questions and voice concerns.[53] Governance and operational concerns were clearly delineated between board members and staff, with board members focusing on long-term concerns and staff focusing on day-to-day operations.[54]

With the technology upgrade, restructured staff and board, and the completion of the stage expansion project, Morris turned his attention to the fourth priority given to him when he was hired: explore new opportunities. Marketing studies conducted at the beginning of the stage expansion project led to additional studies conducted by a Schenectady firm specializing in geographic information systems (GISs). Analysis revealed that much of the Proctors audience was made up of people from outside the city of Schenectady. The board knew that in order to survive and flourish, Proctors would need to become known as the arts and culture destination of the Capital Region. The time for strategic planning had come.

Previous planning practices had included creating a budget with projected outcomes from shows and an outline of staff responsibilities but did not include specific goals and objectives. Morris and the board wanted to create a simple plan with goals and strategies that would cover the next three to five years.[55] A consultant organized a strategic planning session in 2007, and in 2009 the strategic planning committee was formed.

The committee formalized the strategic planning process. Morris created a budget and a plan of implementation that could be used to measure personnel productivity. The board created a three-year plan that included clearly outlined goals and objectives. The first year included a hard budget and plan, while the second and third years consisted of conservative, realistic plans of what Proctors hoped could be achieved.[56] The plan would be assessed each year and adjustments made to reflect changes in the environment.[57]

The new strategic planning process yielded the first change in mission since ACTS's founding in 1977. The original mission read: "The Mission of the Arts Center & Theatre of Schenectady is to provide a diverse program of excellent performing arts events, to restore and preserve the beautiful Proctor's Theatre, to serve as a cultural center for the Capital Region and, to the extent that resources and the Certificate of Incorporation permit, support activities that contribute to the economic development and quality of life in the region."

The new mission better defined what the institution hoped to achieve: "Through arts and community leadership, Proctors will be a catalyst for excellence in education, sustained economic development, and civic engagement to enhance the quality of life in the Capital Region."

By shifting the focus from programming to arts and community leadership, the new mission statement embraced Proctors's role as an economic and cultural force in the region.[58] Throughout its history, Proctors had always been a community center. Morris envisioned Proctors as the "community's living room," and the new mission statement brought Proctors closer to that goal.[59]

Ultimately, the strategic plan covered four areas of growth: economic redevelopment, civic engagement, excellence in education, and financial goals. With a new mission in place, Morris and Proctors moved forward on accomplishing objectives in the four areas of growth.

Economic Development

Morris, the board, Metroplex, and the city of Schenectady knew Proctors could be an economic development powerhouse and key to the revitalization of downtown. Jay Street, a side street perpendicular to Proctors, was one of the first redevelopment projects. When Morris arrived at Proctors, much of the street was vacant. He discussed the possibility of creating a master lease of all the storefronts on Jay Street with the board. Proctors would rent all storefronts on the street and then subrent the spaces to art groups and businesses. Once the leases were filled, Proctors would transfer the leases back to the building owners. The board and the landlords of the Jay Street buildings accepted the proposal, and Proctors signed an agreement to rent all of the storefronts. Within months, all of the stores were filled with tenants.[60]

Morris established relationships with local business owners and city and county officials and kept them abreast of projects that Proctors wanted to pursue. Eventually, these informal conversations turned into weekly meetings during which the group discussed issues that could affect organizations in the city. During one meeting, Morris learned that the Hampton Inn was having difficulty installing a garbage pad. The hotel was required to install the pad, but the installation would eliminate enough guest parking spaces that the Hampton Inn would not be able to guarantee its franchise at the location. Morris realized that Proctors had space for a garbage compactor. He researched the cost of installing a compactor that could serve both the theater and the neighborhood and developed a proposal that included a recycling project and a fee structure for neighborhood businesses. Neighboring businesses supported the project, the Hampton Inn retained its parking spots, and Proctors was able to aid the community while decreasing its own operating costs.

Civic Engagement

Morris often encouraged his staff to actively seek out how Proctors might have an impact in the community.[61] For example, Morris learned that shopkeepers on Jay Street were concerned about vagrancy, so he encouraged his staff to find out what was happening. They soon realized that the "vagrants" were homeless residents of the city. In response, Proctors worked with the Schenectady City Mission to create the Ambassador Program, in which Proctors employed the residents as greeters and ushers. Within months of implementing the Ambassador program, reports of vagrancy on Jay Street disappeared.[62]

Morris and Proctors actively pursued programming that would appeal to the various communities Proctors served. Under Morris, Proctors's reputation as a center for the community brought in people from often underrepresented communities, such as the Latino and Guianese communities who came to Proctors to collaborate and use the space. They often brought films they wished to present in the theater or came to use Proctors's resources, such as public access television.

In 2010, Proctors obtained the rights from the Schenectady Access Council to provide public access television. By taking over the public access television service, SACC-TV, Proctors accomplished several things. First, Proctors received revenue from licensing fees and Time Warner. Second, Proctors was able to tie the channels to its growing education department, and third, SACC-TV enhanced Proctors's regional image. The Schenectady Access Council initially agreed to lease the rights for six months, but eventually, the city gave Proctors the license to manage public access, education, and government TV channels. Renamed Open Stage Media, Proctors received $100,000 a year from Time Warner Cable from surcharges to customers.[63] The channel was moved from its location on Broadway to the Proctors building. Morris saw the move as a way to "deepen and enrich a sense of responsibility for what's happening around us." Both the small staff that ran SACC-TV and the long-running program *Schenectady Today* were retained.[64]

While Proctors expanded programming to become the region's living room, it was the potential collapse of a local equity theater that brought Proctors closer to the goal of regionalization. Carlstrom and board member Anthony Bifaro were also on the board of the local repertory theater, Capital Rep, or Cap Rep, which was based in nearby Albany. The theater itself was in good condition, but debt was increasing and the theater was in danger of closing. If Cap Rep closed, the Capital Region would be the largest area in New York without a presenting organization.[65]

In 2009, Cap Rep and Proctors explored the possibility of developing a relationship. While the initial talks led nowhere, conversations continued at the board level and between Morris and Cap Rep's artistic director, Maggie Mancinelli-Cahill.[66] These talks intensified as Cap Rep's financial situation worsened. Morris and Cap Rep knew immediate action was needed or the region was in danger of losing its only repertory theater.[67]

In July 2010, formal discussions resumed, and the boards of both organizations created task forces to discuss a merger. On the positive side, Cap Rep's ticket sales were good and the two institutions had many similar interests and educational programs that could be aligned. However, concerns about assuming debt, overuse of the Proctors staff, and

potential clashes in cultures and personalities kept the groups from final-
izing the merger. Morris asked both boards to allow him to run Cap Rep
for six months, giving both sides time to reach an agreement.[68]

The New York Council of Nonprofits (NYCON) facilitated talks which
revealed that as long as Cap Rep carried debt, a merger would not be
possible. Morris, using a $250,000 grant awarded to Cap Rep, settled
$500,000 in payables by returning fifty cents on the dollar, leaving only
the $350,000 bank note to contend with.[69] With a large portion of the debt
resolved, a management deal was struck. Proctors would manage the
back office (executive and financial management, box office services,
marketing, and development) for Cap Rep, and though a merger was off
the table at the time, Proctors could, with the consent of Cap Rep, enter
into a merger at any time it deemed appropriate. Morris would become
the chief administrative officer, and the deal could be terminated within
ninety days by Proctors.[70]

The results of the management agreement were positive. Cap Rep
added no new debt in the first year of the merger and ended the year in
the black, and Proctors became a larger player in the Capital Region.
Despite worries that Proctors's philanthropy would be affected, fund-
raising for both institutions improved, and Proctors found that many
previous donors who were inactive resumed giving. Donors supported
the collaboration of arts groups, and the relationship proved to be a boon
in creating better relations with donors in Albany.[71] Although Morris
initially supported a full merger, he was pleased with the arrangement
because it was reproducible. If an arts institution needed assistance, a
similar arrangement could be implemented.

Providing assistance to other nonprofit arts groups was a key element
of Proctors's strategic plan, and Morris found other ways to assist groups
in need. For example, Proctors provided use of its ticketing system, Theater Manager, for free to nonprofits. In lieu of payment, a surcharge was
added when customers purchased tickets. Proctors could also provide
printing and advertising services to nonprofits, acting as an agency and
taking advantage of the discounts on advertising they received.[72]

Excellence in Education

Another advantage of the management agreement with Cap Rep was
the ability to combine the resources of both institutions' education departments. Prior to Morris's arrival, educational programming was limited. The long-running School Days program offered tickets to students for
shows that were often tied to the curriculum.

As budget cuts reduced the number of students coming to Proctors to
see shows and programming, new programs were developed to bring the
arts to students in a variety of ways and in a variety of places. For example, The Open Eye Media program had three components. The Media

Works program allowed students at Schenectady High School and Discovery Academy at Albany High School to integrate media arts into the global history and English language arts Common Core curriculum. The after-school program for middle school students was held at Proctors's Open Stage Media studios. Students used their creativity and developed organizational skills by working in teams to create a program. The Training Institute was a monthly program that taught media arts skills to the public.[73] A School of Arts was also established, something Morris had envisioned when he was first hired. Artistic talent from visiting Broadway shows helped students develop performance skills by offering different courses for various age levels. Cap Rep's Summer Theater at the Rep (STAR) gave students the opportunity to work with theater professionals for the summer.[74] Proctors procured funding for many of the programs through various corporate sponsors and programming expanded to meet the needs of schools in Schenectady and beyond.

Many of these projects were funded through the BOCES system in New York, which helps equalize funding to school programs when two school districts collaborate on a project. After a program has run for a year, depending on the disparity of funding between the two districts, BOCES will fund up to 90 percent of a project the following year. Proctors funded many of the media arts teachers it brought into schools by paying for their salaries during the first year, provided the schools would use all of the following years' BOCES funding to pay for the teachers. Proctors would continue to pay the remaining 10 percent. Morris was able to convince donors to pay for these positions, ensuring the students would enjoy increased exposure to the arts.[75]

Financial Goals

Proctors pursued a mix of revenues from traditional and innovative sources. The theater continued to offer its classic variety of programs, which made up a majority of its revenue. Broadway shows and musicals ran on the main stage while movies and smaller productions used the new GE I-Werks Theatre. In 2006, working with the Independent Producers Network (IPN), Morris brought in new Broadway and independently produced shows as well as entertainment acts. As Morris was strengthening relations with IPN, he expanded the programming by investing in Elephant Eye and Five Cent Productions. Elephant Eye was a group of five large theaters that worked together to produce shows for their theaters, while Five Cent Productions was a group of smaller theaters that were junior partners to Elephant Eye. Five Cent Productions guaranteed the product, provided better deals for the shows, and produced profit if the show succeeded.[76]

Proctors also began management of the coffee shop located in Robb Alley. The coffee shop was originally operated by the Muddy Cup, a local chain of coffee shops. Proctors bought out the lease for the location when the company slowly started closing its branches. Requests for proposals (RFPs) were issued for someone to manage the shop, but Philip wanted to maintain ownership of the café. The board determined that as long as the shop was economically feasible, it could stay in Proctors's control.[77] Dubbed Apostrophe, a play on the lost apostrophe in the Proctors name, the coffee shop allowed Proctors to have better control of its space and the experience it wanted visitors to have when coming to the theater.[78]

In late 2011, Proctors seized an opportunity to buy out Sherwin-Williams from the partnership. The buyout was precipitated by a technicality; neither Morris nor the board realized that the federal government considered the New York State property tax credit Proctors received to be income. As a result, Sherwin-Williams could give Proctors only fifty-five cents on the dollar instead of the traditional eighty-five cents. This loss of revenue cost Proctors $300,000 per year. To resolve the issue, Proctors found the optimum time to buy out Sherwin-Williams in December 2011. At this time, Proctors was still able to receive the credit. However, since Proctors no longer needed the tax credit (the relationship with Sherwin-Williams ended), it was able to get the money in the form of a check instead. Proctors borrowed money from the endowment fund to pay off Sherwin-Williams, and the check compensated Proctors for the short-term loan.[79]

With the Sherwin-Williams partnership terminated and the Cap Rep relationship fully operational, Proctors began to look to the future. Morris and the board decided to eliminate lingering expenses left from the expansion, build working capital, expand the growing endowment, and create a fund to pursue entrepreneurial opportunities and renovations. The North Group conducted confidential interviews with fifty-two regional leaders to determine their opinion of Proctors and their capacity and propensity to give.[80] Based on the results, the group determined that Proctors could raise over $16 million for a capitalization campaign and further recommended that the board raise $400,000 in seed money to pay for campaign expenses.

Morris knew large amounts of money had been raised by local hospitals and educational institutions and felt that Proctors could be the first large cultural nonprofit to do so. Despite Morris's optimism, there was some concern whether a cultural nonprofit could raise such a large amount of money. Still, the board felt that in order for Proctors to succeed in the future, it needed to operate on more than a "shoestring" budget. Trusting in Morris and his staff's abilities, the board moved ahead.[81] The initial goal was met, and the campaign was under way.

EPILOGUE

Proctors is now known nationally as a leader in the arts and culture field, the direct result of Philip Morris's entrepreneurial leadership coupled with the support of the proactive board of directors. Many arts institutions call on Morris and his staff seeking advice.[82] For example, as the Proctors capital campaign was being organized, a new arts institution reached out to Proctors for assistance, the Universal Preservation Hall (UPH) in Saratoga Springs, New York, an old restored church operated by a group of volunteers. UPH was looking for support to finish restoration of the site and manage the organization in order to host "Proctors-like" events at the facility.[83] True to his entrepreneurial vision and community focus, Morris saw the potential relationship with UPH as a way to break down the man-made constructs that divided the cities in the Capital Region, which Morris described "as a suburb surrounded by cities . . . rather than a city surrounded by cities."[84] By listening, reaching out to multiple constituencies, focusing on innovative, collaborative win-win solutions to diverse problems, in short, by becoming the "community's living room," Proctors has succeeded in becoming the largest cultural institution in the Capital Region and a driving force for economic revitalization.

NOTES

1. "F. F. Proctor," Proctors Theatre, accessed November 10, 2012, http://www.proctors.org/ff-proctor.
2. "An Extended History of Proctors: Part I," Proctors Theatre, accessed November 10, 2012, http://www.proctors.org/extended-history1.
3. "An Extended History of Proctors: Part I."
4. "F. F. Proctor," Proctors Theatre, accessed November 10, 2012, http://www.proctors.org/ff-proctor.
5. John Marcille, "ACT Board Votes to Take Proctors," *Schenectady Gazette*, May 24, 1978.
6. "An Extended History of Proctors: Part II," Proctors Theatre, accessed November 10, 2012, http://www.proctors.org/extended-history2.
7. Karen Johnson, interview by author, November 2012.
8. Peg Churchill Wright, "Proctor's Theater Will Mark Five Years of Expansion Tomorrow," *Schenectady Gazette*, January 2, 1984.
9. Churchill Wright, "Proctor's Theater Will Mark Five Years."
10. Peg Churchill Wright, "Proctor's Theatre Layoffs Cut More Than Half the Staff," *Schenectady Gazette*, June 1, 1988.
11. Peg Churchill Wright, "Proctor's Board Gets Panel Report on How to Ensure Theater's Future," *Schenectady Gazette*, August 31, 1988.
12. Karen Johnson, interview by author, November 2012; Churchill Wright, "Proctor'sProctor's Theatre Layoffs."
13. Karen Johnson, interview by author, November 2012.
14. Churchill Wright, "Proctor's Board Gets Panel Report."
15. Lionel Barthold, interview by author, October 2012.

16. Peg Churchill Wright, "Proctor's Creates a New, Smaller Board," *Schenectady Gazette*, October 19, 1988.

17. Peg Churchill Wright, "New Proctor's Season High Schein Priority," *Schenectady Gazette*, August 27, 1988.

18. Karen Johnson, interview by author, November 2012.

19. Churchill Wright, "New Proctor's Season High Schein Priority."

20. Peg Churchill Wright, "Proctor's Board Expects $150,000 Surplus for Year," *Schenectady Gazette*, January 17, 1989.

21. Peg Churchill Wright, "Proctor's Likely to Reach Goal of Fund-Raiser," *Schenectady Gazette*, April 1, 1989.

22. Peg Churchill Wright, "Proctor's Head Sees Surplus, Debt Reduction," *Schenectady Gazette*, May 12, 1989; Lionel Barthold, interview with author, October 2012.

23. Lionel Barthold, interview by author, October 2012.

24. Bill Rice, "Admirers Recall Gloria Lemere, Who Helped Turn Proctors Around," *Daily Gazette*, August 21, 2001.

25. Minutes, Proctors Board of Directors (Schenectady, NY: May 1999).

26. Minutes, Proctors Board of Directors (Schenectady, NY: September 2001).

27. Rick Carlstrom, interview by author, November 2012.

28. Dan Sheehan, interview by author, November 2012.

29. Walter Robb, interview by author, October 2012.

30. "About Us," Schenectady Metroplex Development Authority, accessed November 12, 2012, http://www.schenectadymetroplex.org/about.php.

31. Philip Morris, interview by author, October 2012.

32. Richard Carlstrom, interview by author, November 2012.

33. Richard Carlstrom, interview by author, November 2012.

34. Dan Sheehan, interview by author, November 2012.

35. Minutes, Proctors Board of Directors (Schenectady, NY: September 2002, December 2004).

36. Proctors Expansion Project floor plans (Schenectady, NY: Proctors Theatre, 2005).

37. Philip Morris, "Proctors Theater," presentation given at the Cooperstown Graduate Program, Cooperstown, NY, April 17, 2013.

38. Dan Sheehan, interview by author, November 2012.

39. Dan Sheehan, interview by author, November 2012.

40. Philip Morris, interview by author, October 2012.

41. Philip Morris, interview by author, October 2012; Philip Morris, "Proctors Theater."

42. Dan Sheehan, interview by author, November 2012.

43. Philip Morris, "Proctors Theater."

44. "Narrative about Proctors" (Schenectady, NY: Proctors Theatre, 2008).

45. Philip Morris, interview by author, October 2012.

46. Philip Morris, interview by author, October 2012.

47. Philip Morris, interview by author, October 2012.

48. Minutes, Proctors Board of Directors (Schenectady, NY: July 2002).

49. Philip Morris, interview by author, October 2012.

50. Minutes, Proctors Board of Directors (Schenectady, NY: July 2007).

51. Lionel Barthold, interview by author, October 2012.

52. Minutes, Proctors Board of Directors (Schenectady, NY: June 2007).

53. Richard Carlstrom, interview by author, November 2012.

54. Anthony Mashuta, conversation with author, October 2012.

55. Minutes, Proctors Board of Directors (Schenectady, NY: October 2007).

56. Richard Carlstrom, interview by author, October 2012.

57. Richard Carlstrom, interview by author, October 2012.

58. Philip Morris, "Proctors Theater."

59. Gregg Millet, "Proctors Un-Gala, Part I," video, 30:00, from Proctors' UN-Gala event honoring Philip Morris' ten-year anniversary, filmed September 15, 2012, http://www.youtube.com/watch?v=OYhWUM5A-Os.

60. Philip Morris, interview by author, October 2012; Philip Morris, "Proctors Theater."

61. Philip Morris, interview by author, October 2012; Philip Morris, "Proctors Theater."

62. Gregg Millet, "Philip Morris Talks to GenNext," video, 30:07, from a GenNext event at Proctors Theatre, filmed February 2011, http://blip.tv/greggmillett/philip-morris-talks-to-gennext-4772589.

63. Minutes, Proctors Board of Directors (Schenectady, NY: November 2009–January 2010).

64. Lauren Stanforth, "Proctors Lifts Curtain on TV Plan," *Times Union*, October 21, 2009, http://www.timesunion.com/local/article/Proctors-lifts-curtain-on-TV-plan-5560 47.php.

65. Anthony Mashuta, conversation with author, October 2012.

66. Richard Carlstrom, interview by author, October 2012.

67. Philip Morris, interview by author, October 2012.

68. Minutes, Proctors Board of Directors (Schenectady, NY: December 2010); Philip Morris, interview by author, October 2012.

69. Minutes, Proctors Board of Directors (Schenectady, NY: October–December 2010); Philip Morris, interview by author, October 2012.

70. Minutes, Proctors Board of Directors (Schenectady, NY: October–December 2010); Richard Carlstrom, interview by author, October 2012.

71. Lionel Barthold, interview by author, October 2012.

72. Philip Morris, interview by author, October 2012.

73. Minutes, Proctors Board of Directors (Schenectady, NY: May 2010); "Open Eye," Proctors Theatre, accessed January 3, 2013, http://www.proctors.org/education/open-eye.

74. Anthony Bifaro, interview by author, October 2012; School of Performing Arts brochure.

75. Philip Morris, "Proctors Theater."

76. Minutes, Proctors Board of Directors (Schenectady, NY: May 2006).

77. "Apostrophe Café at Proctors," Schenectady Metroplex Development Authority, accessed October 17, 2012, http://www.schenectadymetroplex.org/newsArticle.php?id=289; Minutes, Proctors Board of Directors (Schenectady, NY: February 2011).

78. Anthony Mashuta, conversation with author, October 2012.

79. Philip Morris, interview by author, October 2012; Minutes, Proctors Board of Directors (Schenectady, NY: December 2011).

80. Proctors Theatre, *Securing Proctors' Future: The Next Act* (Schenectady: Proctors Theatre, 2012).

81. Minutes, Proctors Board of Directors (Schenectady, NY: October 2011).

82. Lionel Barthold, interview by author, December 2011.

83. Minutes, Proctors Board of Directors (Schenectady, NY: June 2012).

84. Philip Morris, interview by author, October 2012.

BIBLIOGRAPHY

Arts Center Theater of Schenectady. Board Meeting Minutes. Schenectady: Proctors Theater, 1990–2012.

Badal, Sangeeta, and Joe Streur. "What Drives Entrepreneurs to Win." *Gallup Business Journal*. Accessed September 16, 2012. http://businessjournal.gallup.com/content/156956/drives-entrepreneurs-win.aspx?utm_sour#2.

Barthold, Lionel. Interview by author. Lake George, NY, October 19, 2012.

Bifaro, Anthony. Telephone interview by author. October 30, 2012.

Carlstrom, Rick. Telephone interview by author. November 4, 2012.

Churchill Wright, Peg. "Madden Resigns Post at Proctors; Board Begins New Director Search." *Schenectady Gazette*, July 15, 1988.

———. "New Proctor's Season High Schein Priority." *Schenectady Gazette*, August 27, 1988.

———. "Proctor's Board Creates New, Smaller Board." *Schenectady Gazette*, October 19, 1988.

———. "Proctor's Board Expects $150,000 Surplus for Year." *Schenectady Gazette*, January 17, 1989.

———. "Proctor's Board Gets Panel Report on How to Ensure Theater's Future." *Schenectady Gazette*, August 31, 1988.

———. "Proctor's Head Sees Surplus, Debt Reduction." *Schenectady Gazette*, May 12, 1989.

———. "Proctor's Likely to Reach Goal of Fund-Raiser." *Schenectady Gazette*, April 1, 1989.

———. "Proctor's Theater Will Mark Five Years of Expansion Tomorrow." *Schenectady Gazette*, January 2, 1984.

———. "Proctor's Theatre Layoffs Cut More Than Half the Staff." *Schenectady Gazette*, June 1, 1988.

D'Agenese, Elena. "CEG 2010 Annual Meeting—Philip Morris." Filmed December 6, 2010. YouTube video, 8:18. http://www.youtube.com/watch?v=KvFQvOpPfZQ.

DeMasi, Michael. "Proctors Selling 440 State St. to Tech Company." *Business Review*, July 14, 2010. Accessed September 7, 2012. http://www.bizjournals.com/albany/stories/2010/07/12/daily25.html.

Dym, Barry, and Harry Hutson. *Leadership in Nonprofit Organizations.*Thousand Oaks, CA: SAGE, 2005.

Hipp, Marilyn. "Proctor's Theatre Names CEO." *Daily Gazette*, January 8, 2002.

Holck, Mary D. "Proctor's to Undergo Restoration This Summer." *Daily Gazette*, March 1, 1991.

Johnson, Karen. Interview by author. Schenectady, NY, November 6, 2012.

Marcille, John. "ACT Board Votes to Take Proctors." *Schenectady Gazette*, May 24, 1978. Accessed September 6, 2012. http://news.google.com/newspapers?nid=1917&dat=19780524&id=LBYxAAAAIBAJ&sjid=BOEFAAAAIBAJ&pg=2891,8688854.

Mashuta, Anthony. Conversation with author. Latham, NY, October 18, 2012.

Millet, Gregg. "Philip Morris Talks to GenNext." Filmed February 2011. Video, 30:07. http://blip.tv/greggmillett/philip-morris-talks-to-gennext-4772589.

———. "Proctors Un-Gala, Part I." Filmed September 15, 2012. Video, 30:00. http://www.youtube.com/watch?v=OYhWUM5A-Os.

Morris, Philip. Interview by author. Cooperstown, NY, October 31, 2012.

———. "Proctors Theater." Presentation given at the Cooperstown Graduate Program in Cooperstown, NY, April 17, 2013.

Proctors Theatre. "2011 Strategic Plan." Schenectady, NY: Proctors Theatre, 2010.

———. "An Extended History of Proctors: Part I." Accessed November 10, 2012. http://www.proctors.org/extended-history1.

———. "An Extended History of Proctors: Part II." Accessed November 10, 2012. http://www.proctors.org/extended-history2.

———. "F. F. Proctor." Accessed November 10, 2012. http://www.proctors.org/ff-proctor.

———. "Narrative about Proctors." Schenectady, NY: Proctors Theatre, 2008.

———. "Proctor's Visitor Center, Something for Everyone Downtown." Accessed October 17, 2012. http://www.proctors.org/news/2012/06/proctors-visitors-center-something-everyone-downtown.

———. *Securing Proctors' Future: The Next Act.* Schenectady, NY: Proctors Theatre, 2012.

Rice, Bill. "Admirers Recall Gloria Lemere, Who Helped Turn Proctors Around." *Daily Gazette*, August 21, 2001. http://news.google.com/newspapers?nid=1957&dat=20010821&id=xnMhAAAAIBAJ&sjid=pogFAAAAIBAJ&pg=5952,4471909.

Robb, Walter. Telephone interview by author. October 18, 2012.

Schenectady Metroplex Development Authority. "About Us." Accessed November 12, 2012. http://www.schenectadymetroplex.org/about.php.

———. "Apostrophe Café at Proctors." Accessed October 17, 2012. http://www.schenectadymetroplex.org/newsArticle.php?id=289.

———. "KeyBank Sells State Street Branch to Proctors under Market Price for Community Gathering Space." March 3, 2010. Accessed September 6, 2012. http://www.schenectadymetroplex.org/newsArticle.php?id=185.

Sheehan, Dan. Telephone interview by author. November 5, 2012.

Smith, Stanley. Conversation with author. Schenectady, NY, October 18, 2012.

Spear, Ellen. "Fostering Innovation." Session at the New England Museum Association Conference, Burlington, VT, November 8, 2012.

Stanforth, Lauren. "Proctors Lifts Curtain on TV Plan." *Times Union*, October 21, 2009. Accessed September 7, 2012. http://www.timesunion.com/local/article/Proctors-lifts-curtain-on-TV-plan-556047.php.

FOUR

America's River

The Reinvention of the Mississippi River Museum

Jerome Enzler

From 1992 to 2003, the Dubuque County Historical Society and its Mississippi River Museum in Dubuque, Iowa, were part of a riverfront development effort called "America's River." The museum and its partners raised $57 million for museum expansion and endowment and $131 million in leveraged investments. This metamorphosis changed nearly every facet of the Mississippi River Museum, including increases in attendance, memberships, staff, facilities' size, outdoor interpretive space acreage, and the endowment.[1] This story of reinvention from county historical society to national museum was made possible through vision, savvy development and fund-raising, and a focus on building critical local, regional, national, and federal partnerships.

INTRODUCTION

Dubuque is located on the Mississippi River at the junction of Iowa, Wisconsin, and Illinois, and its history is closely tied to the Mississippi River. French-Canadian fur trader and lead miner Julien Dubuque lived there with the Meskwaki Indians from 1788 until his death in 1810. From 1810 to 1832, the Meskwaki extracted the lead ore with little interference from Euro-American miners. The Black Hawk War in 1832 led to the removal of the Meskwaki people, and Dubuque's mines were opened for occupation by American citizens on June 1, 1833.[2]

Figure 4.1.   National Mississippi River Museum & Aquarium, Backwater Marsh Exhibit.

In later years, Dubuque's economy was built upon agriculture, log milling, meat packing, boat building, education, manufacturing, health care, and tourism.[3] By 2000, people of Irish and German heritage made up almost 98 percent of Dubuque's population of 57,669 people.[4]

The Dubuque County Historical Society was incorporated in 1950 as a private, nonprofit Iowa corporation with a purpose "to discover, collect, and preserve . . . any and all materials which may establish or illustrate the history of this county, state or adjoining states."[5] From 1950 to 1964, the society focused on sponsoring meetings and public programs, preservation of historic structures in the county, and collection of oral histories, archives, and library resources.

In 1964 the society established its first museum, the Mathias Ham House, located in an Italian Villa–style house constructed in 1856.[6] Under the leadership of volunteer Helen Mercer and other board members, and with the acquisition of the collections of the Richard Herrmann Museum of Natural History in 1965 (a private Dubuque museum kept in the home of Richard and Lena Herrmann from 1871 to 1956), collections grew exponentially.[7] The society worked diligently to save historic structures and added a log cabin, a caboose, and a one-room schoolhouse to the Ham House grounds over the next ten years. In 1977, membership was approximately three hundred individuals or families, the annual budget was approximately ten thousand dollars, and annual attendance was three thousand people.[8]

The society's second museum, initially called the Fred Woodward Upper Mississippi Riverboat Museum, opened to the public in 1980 with a focus on the history of the five-state region of the Upper Mississippi. As a result of capital campaigns in 1979, 1984, and 1989, the society and its museums grew into an organization of thirteen full-time staff, with an audience of seventy thousand people, an annual budget of approximately $750,000, and endowment of $200,000.[9]

Still, the museum's largest growth was yet to come. In 1993, society president William Woodward, in ill health, revealed his intention to name the museum as the residual beneficiary of his estate. The gift was estimated at two million dollars, ten times larger than the largest gift the society had ever received. When Woodward passed away on August 12, 1995,[10] his gift set in motion a series of events which would forever transform the museum and the society.

REINVENTION OF A MUSEUM

Planning for the establishment of a river museum in Dubuque began when the Dubuque Boat and Boiler Works closed in 1971, after a 102-year history of building steamboats and towboats.[11] Through the inspiration of civic leader Wayne A. Norman Sr., the society began planning for the Riverboat Museum in 1975 with a self-study and national search of comparable museums funded by the National Endowment for the Humanities.[12] Robert and Ruth Kehl, operators of the local river excursion boat, donated a waterfront warehouse building,[13] and the Woodward Foundation issued a challenge pledge of $200,000, if $600,000 could be raised.[14] Jerry Enzler was hired by the society in 1977 as curator of the Mathias Ham House and was later named director of museums for both the existing Mathias Ham House and the emerging Upper Mississippi Riverboat Museum.

A fund drive from 1979 to 1981 raised $1.1 million.[15] In 1980, the museum acquired a historic steamboat, the *William M. Black*, and in 1982 opened the first displays in the Fred W. Woodward Upper Mississippi Riverboat Museum building. The museum's geographic scope included the five states of the Upper Mississippi River—Minnesota, Wisconsin, Iowa, Illinois, and Missouri.

A $1.2 million fund-raising effort was conducted in 1984 to complete the exhibits in the waterfront freight house building, establish a $200,000 endowment to support operations, and lay the groundwork for an organization called the National Rivers Hall of Fame, which would focus on people of all the rivers in the United States.[16] The museum decided, for the near future, not to amass large collections of objects from all of America's rivers. Rather, the Hall of Fame would engage in educational outreach with programs, publications, and small biographical exhibits about people of America's rivers.[17]

In 1986, the board addressed the name of the riverfront museum complex, which by then included the Fred W. Woodward Upper Mississippi Riverboat Museum, the Steamboat *William M. Black*, and the National Rivers Hall of Fame. A new name was needed to create a consistent marketing presence and to indicate the museum's reach beyond the Upper Mississippi and beyond riverboats. After thorough discussion, the board approved the name "Mississippi River Museum" for the entire river museum complex.[18]

From 1989 to 1991, a third capital fund drive increased the endowment to $600,000 and raised $3.5 million to create an exhibition facility in a shared building with a riverboat casino.[19] Previous expansions by the museum had resulted in significant increases in attendance, but this expansion did not meet expectations. While the casino development attracted large numbers of people, most of these visitors were not museum attendees. In 1992, the museum conducted an informal survey which revealed that only one in ten people who were entering the casino had intentions of visiting the museum or were aware of its existence, even though the entry doors were almost side by side. By contrast, nine out of ten visitors to the Fenelon Place Elevator, a funicular located four blocks away, were aware of the museum and had visited it or were intending to visit it on that trip.[20] Board and staff concluded that because of the overwhelming number of casino visitors and the construction of parking facilities surrounding the museum, the museum had lost its "sense of place."[21]

The failure of the museum's latest expansion to increase attendance and the perceived loss of sense of place motivated the board and staff to analyze museum offerings. From 1992 to 1997, the museum participated in a series of planning exercises which helped form its future, in terms of both scope and expansion. As a result, the society's mission was revised to address the geographic scope of the society's museums and to emphasize the importance of environmental concerns and global perspectives. The revised mission statement detailed the society's mission "to explore, research, preserve, and interpret, for present and future generations, the history of diverse people and cultures of Dubuque County, the Mississippi River, and the rivers of the United States." An additional statement read, "The Society accomplishes its mission through dedication to scholarly research, the preservation of material culture, and the presentation of provocative, meaningful, and educational exhibits, programs, and publications, within a regional, national, and global perspective."[22]

During this period, the museum also participated in a MAP III Public Dimension Assessment, funded by the Institute of Museum Services. The assessment included a focus group of adults, an analysis from two visiting museum professionals, people-on-the-street interviews, and a focus group of schoolchildren from grades one through eight. President Woodward wanted to build a hands-on discovery center, and the museum's curatorial perspective and training all pointed toward history as well, but in the student focus group, student after student expressed interest in the environment of the river. Finally, an eighth-grader said he wanted to know about the history of the river—the age of the fish in the river and the age of the river itself. The museum realized that further reflection about the focus for its new discovery center was needed.

With two grants from the National Endowment for the Humanities (NEH), the museum engaged in a one-year self-study and a two-year planning grant to develop the concepts for the expanded museum. This included traveling to other river museums and working with a team of national and local scholars to investigate approaches for the Mississippi River Museum. The museum had a growing interest in environmental history. From engineered locks and dam systems to the tremendous force of the river in the devastating flood of 1993, environmental history and the cultural history of the Mississippi were intermingled, just as human and natural systems along the river were intertwined.

Thomas Morain, director of interpretation at Living History Farms in Urbandale, Iowa, suggested that project consultants were too close to the Mississippi and that they should, in their minds, get on a plane and go to the Amazon River. As they arrived on the shores of the Amazon, he asked what they wanted to know, recording their queries on a flip chart. The questions related to the river's size, creatures, boats and cargo, and people present and past. Morain halted the exercise and noted that although they were all historians, they did not ask about the history of the people of the Amazon until their fifth question. The history of the people of the river was essential, but it was not the only story to be told.[23]

These three factors—the overwhelming interest in the natural world by the public, the environmental history approach which challenged historians to treat the Mississippi as an artifact whose changes should be interpreted, and the questions about the Amazon—led the museum to reexamine the scope of its development for the Mississippi River Museum. Would the museum address the historical questions that its staff was trained to address based on vocation and training, or would the museum explore all aspects of the Mississippi River—future as well as past, environment as well as history? The decision was made to tell the story of the environment of the river and the history of its people, past and future.[24] Ironically, the discussion had come full circle. The environment of the Mississippi was originally planned as the first exhibit when the original Upper Mississippi River Museum opened in 1980, only to be voted down by board members who feared that dead fish (floaters) would mar visitors' first impressions of the museum.

Woodward's last annual meeting as president of the society was January 9, 1995. In his address, "Vision 2000," Woodward described the shared vision for the expanded museum, saying, "The new River Discovery Center will be about how the Mississippi affects people and how people affect the Mississippi River. It will be 'hands-on,' colorful, with highly interactive exhibits. The exhibits will be so enticing that neither parents nor children will be able to keep their hands off. Furthermore, there will be no museum like this anywhere up or down the Mississippi River."[25] Eight months later, on August 12, 1995, Woodward passed away. Woodward's gift was estimated to be $1.8 million, with one half designated for new facilities and one half designated for endowment. The time for conceptual planning was over. The board and staff felt an urgency to spend Woodward's bequest wisely and expeditiously.

State senator Mike Connolly agreed to coordinate an effort to secure funding from the state of Iowa. He and his colleagues introduced language into a state bill to secure $1 million for the project, granting $500,000 each year for two years to a historical organization that currently held a challenge grant from the NEH. The Mississippi River Museum was the only organization that had achieved the qualifying benchmark. Museum staff presented the bill to both the Democratic and Republican caucuses and received their support. The bill passed both the Iowa Senate and House and was sent to the office of Iowa Governor Terry Branstad for his signature. In 1996, Governor Branstad was visiting Dubuque for the Republican caucus. Local businessman and Branstad supporter R. D. McDonald, who had been a friend of the museum for decades, arranged to drive the governor to the Dubuque airport, along with director Enzler and development director Teri Goodmann. While en route, McDonald told the governor how important this project was and how good it would be for the state. The governor supported the appropriation, and the museum secured $1 million in state funds for the expansion. With Iowa State's support and Woodward's bequest, the museum had almost $3 million in promised funds.

A building committee for the proposed River Discovery Center was formed, consisting of civic and business leaders.[26] Enzler, who had led the museum since its founding and had extensive grant-writing, consulting, and project management experience, directed both the development and the exhibits. Development director Teri Goodmann, who had originally been hired by the society in 1995 as director of marketing, events, and volunteers, coordinated fund-raising. Goodmann had extensive experience in managing political campaigns at the state, city, and county level and had strong relationships with Democratic leaders in the United States Congress. Her experience in community activities and political affairs proved invaluable in advancing the effort on all levels.

The goal was to build a world-class museum to interpret the Mississippi River with a focus on the attitudes that people had held over time towards the river and the technological and cultural systems that altered the river. The building committee met weekly for seven years to plan and implement the museum expansion. In searching for both exhibit designers and architects, the museum found that few firms had experience in both historical and aquatic facilities. The museum hired designers and architects with aquarium experience because of the technical difficulty of aquatic installation and because the museum already had expertise in historical exhibits. The exhibit design team was engaged six months in advance of the architectural team to ensure that the function of the museum would prevail over the form of the building.

The exhibit plan included many historical exhibits as well as aquariums of Mississippi River fish and mammals, a flood table, an erosion table, a wet lab, and an outdoor wetland.[27] The consultants presented options for additional exhibits and visitor experiences as well, and the museum was attracted to those proposals, believing that it ultimately could raise the funds needed. The preliminary estimate for the building and exhibits was $20 million.

When plans were announced that the museum was going to build a $20 million River Discovery Center that included historical exhibits and aquariums, some people singularly focused on the aquariums. NEH scholars made the case that environment cannot be ignored in interpreting the Mississippi River. There was enormous interest in the country about the current state of the river, particularly the lock and dam system on the Upper Mississippi River; structural versus nonstructural approaches to flood protection; and issues such as water quality as it related to both humans and aquatic life. To make the campaign a success, the museum made sure that it emphasized the historical as well as the aquatic exhibits so that people would not focus only on the aquariums.

FORMING THE AMERICA'S RIVER PARTNERSHIP

At the same time that the museum was planning its major expansion, the City of Dubuque and the Dubuque Area Chamber of Commerce were planning to launch their own fund drive for riverfront development. Their goal was to create a river walk and further develop a city riverfront park at the north end of the city, Hawthorne Park. Museum leaders wondered how two riverfront fund drives could be conducted at once. The museum conveyed its perspective to the mayor, city council, city staff, and the leadership of the Dubuque Area Chamber of Commerce, explaining how it would be confusing to potential donors to have two simultaneous fund drives, each focusing on riverfront development. Further, the museum had to rely on gifts and grants to expand its museum, while the city had the ability to tax its citizens to accomplish its goal. This uneasy situation continued without resolution for several months, each side trying to explain its point of view to the other. The city/chamber project was ahead of the museum in its planning; the chamber had already recruited a respected attorney as campaign leader and several community leaders to serve as a campaign cabinet. The museum did not have a community team in place but did have several lead gifts already secured to start the fund drive.

Finally, a compromise was reached. Community support for municipal improvements was important to the city, and voter support was just as important as money. The city agreed that it would be happy with broad community support and $350,000 towards its improvements. The museum needed at least $5 million in private funds locally to construct its expansion. Ultimately, the three groups agreed to join forces under the name "America's River" to collaboratively raise the funds. Plans for the museum and the river walk would proceed under a united fund-raising effort. The museum would focus on its expansion. The chamber, acting on behalf of the city, would focus on the river walk with several public amenities adjacent to the museum and its expansion. Plans for Hawthorne Street riverfront development were deferred. Gifts received would be distributed, after fund-raising expenses, in the ratio that they were needed—7 percent to the chamber/city for the river walk and 93 percent to the museum.[28]

Feasibility Study

In 1997, the museum and the chamber jointly authorized a study to determine the level of public support and fund-raising potential for America's River. Project officials hired the firm of Howard Braren Associates, Inc., of Davenport, Iowa, to conduct the study. Enzler, Goodmann, Chamber of Commerce president Steven Horman, and Convention and Visitors Bureau director Sue Czeshinski led the effort.

The museum and the chamber prepared a case statement that described the project, and designers created visual representations of the major project elements. The case statement projected a total budget of $25 million, $20 million for the museum expansion, and $5 million for the river walk and amenities.[29] Although $25 million was a sizable goal, the case described a strategy to reach that level, and the project already had $6.1 million in hand.[30] Fund-raising counsel suggested that it test a fund-raising goal of $5.35 million locally, an amount large enough to be visionary but not so large that it would scare potential donors away. The remaining $13.65 million would be raised from national and governmental sources.

Community leaders and board members hosted small-group meetings in their homes, and America's River leaders presented the case statement, visuals, and probable costs. Additional public awareness meetings were held regionally in Des Moines and Cedar Rapids. When asked when the new museum would open, the museum replied that it would open when funds were raised; money would not be borrowed for the project. The value of this fund-raising feasibility study was enormous. The study engaged potential donors in a dialogue, introducing them to the project in a nonthreatening way and engaging them initially as advisors, not as donors.

Braren, Mulder, and German Associates also interviewed ninety-seven of these leaders, asking them a series of questions in a confidential setting. Another forty-four leaders responded to a mail survey. Ninety-six percent of respondents, an extraordinarily high rating for a fund-raising feasibility study, supported the project. Seventy-seven percent of persons surveyed said they would make a gift or pledge to the program. Sixty-eight percent of persons interviewed said they would take a volunteer role in the upcoming campaign. Typical comments included: "No organization can do this alone. Having the City and Chamber involved elevates the project to something that is viable. It lends credibility . . ." and "Dubuque is finally taking advantage of its greatest natural resource—the Mississippi River." The feasibility study concluded, "Dubuque is clearly captivated by the possibility of completing America's River. With its tremendous cultural, educational, recreational, environmental and economic benefits, the project is seen as a huge step forward for the City. Leaders are unequivocal in their willingness to move forward with the fund raising program."[31]

Local Fund-Raising

Fund-raising for the local campaign began in 1998 and was organized into multiple phases: advanced giving, leadership, special and general campaigns. Major gifts were solicited throughout the community. More than four hundred public forums were held where America's River was described to potential donors and collaborators.[32]

For the advanced giving phase of the local campaign, America's River secured the support of eighteen civic leaders from major philanthropic, civic, and corporate interests in the community to serve as general chairs. They helped identify and call on major calls of $25,000 and above. Face-to-face calls made to virtually all the major donor prospects resulted in a strong response; gifts began to come in at four to five times more than the donor had ever given to a charitable organization before. When the first $1 million was secured towards the local goal of $5.35 million, the museum held a media conference to announce the donors which made up that $1 million total.[33] Several gifts were ultimately secured at the $50,000 and $100,000 level. Donors at the $25,000 level were attracted by the opportunity to have their names collectively associated with the main channel aquarium.

The leadership phase was targeted for donors giving from $5,000 to $25,000 and thirty leadership chairs volunteered to make calls at this level. The leadership chairs were thoroughly briefed on the project, trained in fund-raising techniques, and provided with office support during their efforts. More than 750 prospects were identified, and they were invited to a launching event on August 24, 1999, aboard the *Celebration Belle* riverboat to publicly begin this phase of the campaign.

To attract volunteers for the special and general campaign, two luncheons were held in December 1999. Over eighty people attended these luncheons and signed up for one of three task forces: fund development, public relations, and marketing. A fifteen-member fund development task force, cochaired by two community leaders, planned a series of twenty-five gatherings in the community. Neighbors invited neighbors to their home for refreshments and a presentation about America's River. This was an effective way to involve people at the grassroots level to introduce and endorse the project. It also helped identify which prospects had strong interest in the project. Party hosts, with the help of America's River staff, followed up with requests for donations.

The twenty-member public relations task force, chaired by a professor of communications at Loras College, developed public service announcements and a national and local media campaign to draw attention to the project.[34] A local songwriter donated his time to write a jingle, and the Dubuque Chorale and Youth Chorus recorded the jingle with studio time donated by a professional recording studio. A campaign slogan was selected: "Educate, Navigate, Recreate, Participate." A speaker's bureau presented the project to various groups in the community. Volunteers created a summer passport of activities and festivals, and several public festivals from May 2000 to October 2000 were dedicated to America's River.[35]

The fifteen-member marketing task force was chaired by a marketing professional from American Trust and Savings Bank. The task force developed a marketing strategy for the general campaign with a target audience of donors projected at a giving level under $5,000. The strategy included donated print, billboard, and radio advertising; direct mail; and publicity and feature articles.[36] The goal was to ensure that every resident of Dubuque received at least six media "hits" about America's River before being asked to contribute. For the direct-mail campaign, a brochure was mailed to 15,000 households with a head of household over twenty-five years of age and a household annual income over $35,000. Donations from the first sixteen respondents paid for the entire cost of printing the brochure.

The local fund-raising effort was successful at all levels. The campaign raised over $6 million, exceeding the fund-raising goal of $5.35 million. These funds were added to $2.3 million in bequests from local donors William Woodward and Helen Everest.

Local, Statewide, and Regional Partnerships

Partnerships were important to the fund-raising program as well as the development of exhibits. The Greater Dubuque Development Corporation, a not-for-profit economic development agency for the Dubuque area, provided leadership in the strategic planning and development of America's River while the Dubuque Area Labor Management Council, a coalition of leaders in both management and labor, served as an advisor, providing an important link between project officials and organized labor and management. The Sac and Fox Tribal Council of Tama, Iowa, worked with America's River to develop exhibits to tell the story of the Meskwaki people and their settlement at Dubuque. Museum planners also collaborated with the regional office of the National Audubon Society, and Audubon ultimately purchased and docked an educational vessel at the museum.

America's River Museum also created important partnerships with educational institutions. The Dubuque Community School District designated the museum as an extended satellite classroom in recognition of the educational impact of the museum. Scholars from Clarke College, Loras College, University of Dubuque, and others assisted with exhibit content.[37] Graceland College in Lamoni, Iowa, was one of several colleges that established a museum internship program.

The museum initiated several efforts to increase relevancy by engaging with the community. The museum established a local chapter of the Friends of the Upper Mississippi River Refuge to work with the other Friends chapters in Winona, Minnesota, La Crosse, Wisconsin, and Savanna, Illinois. The River Discovery Consortium, formed as an organization of environmental groups and citizens, brought together over forty

organizations and thirty individuals to help plan the museum and to
engage in environmental activities. With the help of the consortium, the
Catfish Creek Coalition was organized for the purpose of raising public
awareness about the Catfish Creek watershed and its importance to the
main stem of the river and to inspire people to act as stewards of this
natural resource.[38]

The museum established closer relationships with the departments of
natural resources or conservation in Iowa, Illinois, Wisconsin, Minnesota,
and Missouri. America's River and the museum joined as partners in the
Grand Excursion of 2004, a re-creation of the grand excursion of the
Upper Mississippi in 1854. The museum also became an organizational
member of the Iowa Environmental Council to conserve Iowa's environment and became a partner site of the Silos and Smokestacks Natural
Heritage Area in northeast Iowa.

Finally, the museum founded the Great River Road's Mississippi River Interpretive Center Network, a collaboration of fifty museums and
interpretive centers in ten states along the Mississippi River. The museum participated with all ten states in developing themes for interpretation for the Mississippi River and created an interpretive tool kit for the
river.[39]

National Fund-Raising

At the same time as America's River was raising money locally, museum leaders launched a national fund-raising campaign. Project officials
made repeated trips to St. Louis, Minneapolis, New Orleans, Houston,
Nashville, New York, and Washington, D.C., to lay the foundation for
national giving. Steps taken for national fund-raising included presentations and appearances at national meetings each year and personal presentations to key leaders in the national environmental movement and
the national waterways industry.[40] Through the National Rivers Hall of
Fame, the museum already had a national advisory board and a small but
geographically diverse membership base residing in thirty-five states.
The Hall of Fame had been collecting the history of leaders in river industry, environment, and recreation since 1985, and over time, the museum
developed relationships with national corporate leaders. The Hall of
Fame presented national achievement awards each year to a living person who had made significant contributions to any aspect of the rivers of
America, not only in commerce but in history, writing, and the environment.

To guide the national fund-raising, the museum formed a national
cabinet of leaders to serve as advisors on funding for the River Discovery
Center.[41] This team worked with Enzler and Goodmann as well as Hall
of Fame president Gordon Kilgore, a river historian and fifty-year radio
broadcaster in the Dubuque area, who recorded oral histories of many of

these individuals. The value of the national cabinet was threefold. First, they provided gifts from their personal, corporate, and foundation resources. Second, they opened doors to others who would make gifts to the campaign. Third, they provided significant endorsements, which helped elevate the status of the campaign to a national level. The national fund-raising effort resulted in gifts exceeding $2 million, including a $1 million gift of books, paintings, and a charitable gift annuity to endow the Captain William Bowell River Library.[42]

Federal Partnerships and Support

The museum created a deliberate strategy to develop partnerships with and secure key endorsements from federal agencies. The threefold goal was to raise the profile of the project nationally, access the historic and scientific resources of these agencies, and secure federal funding. For seven years, museum staff and board members, joined by the mayor, city council, city manager, county board of supervisors, and officials from the Chamber of Commerce, traveled to Washington, D.C. to develop partnerships and secure appropriations. US Senators Tom Harkin and Charles Grassley and Congressman Jim Nussle, as well as their staffs, worked tirelessly to advance the project, both in the halls of Congress and with potential supporters.

The US Fish and Wildlife Service signed a twenty-year partnership agreement with the museum to interpret the Upper Mississippi River National Fish and Wildlife Refuge, the nation's longest and most visited refuge, with three million visitors a year. Dubuque is centrally located in the refuge, which is 261 miles long and contains over 194,000 acres in four states—Minnesota, Wisconsin, Iowa, and Illinois.[43]

The US Army Corps of Engineers signed a five-year partnership agreement with the museum, promising the resources of the Mississippi Valley Division of the US Army Corps of Engineers and all six districts on the Mississippi River—St. Paul, Rock Island, St. Louis, Memphis, Vicksburg, and New Orleans.[44]

The US Coast Guard agreed to a three-year partnership memorandum with the museum. This agreement, signed by Admiral Paul Pluta in New Orleans in 2000, provided assistance to the museum's efforts to tell the story of aids to navigation, safety efforts on the river, and the history of boats built at the museum site for the Coast Guard.[45]

The scientists from the US Geological Survey worked with the museum to create the flood-plain model and other exhibits. Over the previous fourteen years, the Geological Survey's Mississippi River Environmental Monitoring Program (EMP) at Onalaska, Wisconsin, had conducted over $100 million of research. Its partnership with the museum allowed the Geological Survey to find a public outlet for this information and allowed the museum to have access to the leading scientific research on the river.

The museum applied for and became a Smithsonian affiliate, one of approximately 120 such affiliate museums in the country.[46] Affiliate status allowed access to collections, programming, curatorial expertise, and collaborative membership programming for the museum.

America's River became one of the key projects in the Federal American Heritage Rivers Program, a White House initiative that included fifty-six communities along the Upper Mississippi River for development, preservation, and interpretation.[47] James Lee Witt, director of the Federal Emergency Management Administration (FEMA), came to Dubuque in 1998 to announce the American Heritage Rivers Program for the Upper Mississippi River.

The museum became a Coastal Ecosystem Learning Center as part of its selection as part of Coastal America, a White House initiative created by executive order of the president. This collaborative, which in 2006 consisted of twenty-two of the leading aquariums and environmental education centers in the country, provided a memorandum of agreement with fourteen different agencies of the federal government to further its educational goals. The museum is the only Coastal Ecosystem Learning Center on the inland rivers of the United States.

National and federal endorsements became an important part of the effort as well. Members of the US Congress had recently formed the Upper Mississippi River Congressional Task Force.[48] Museum officials testified before this congressional caucus, and the caucus provided a letter of support which read, "[W]e would like to share our support for a project we think would be a great asset to the Upper Mississippi River Basin and the entire nation."[49]

Through the efforts of Congressman Jim Nussle, the museum was invited to testify twice before the House Subcommittee on Interior Appropriations. Based on the museum's partnership with the US Fish and Wildlife Service and its Upper Mississippi National Wildlife and Fish Refuge, Congressman Nussle requested funding of $2 million for the museum. This request was to be considered by the House Subcommittee on Interior Appropriations, so the congressman invited Dubuque mayor Duggan and Enzler to testify before the committee.[50] Enzler testified, "The Upper Mississippi Fish and Wildlife Refuge, the nation's longest and busiest refuge, has three million visitors a year, as many as Yellowstone National Park. Yet the Upper Mississippi River Refuge, 261 miles long and bordering four states, has no interpretive center."[51]

Numerous leaders provided valuable endorsements. For example, William Ferris, Chairman of the National Endowment for the Humanities, said in the NEH award of a $500,000 challenge grant, "Going far beyond the scope of most county historical societies, your organization has become a vehicle for telling the big story of the Mississippi River to local, regional, and national audiences."[52] The governors of the five Upper Mississippi River states provided a letter of endorsement in 1999, which stated, "As governors of the five states that share the Upper Mississippi River, we strongly support the development of the first-of-its-kind Upper Mississippi River Interpretive Center to share its bounty with all citizens. . . . The people of our five states are committing $13 million toward this $26 million Center."[53] Through these efforts, federal support for America's River totaled over $11 million.[54]

VISION IOWA

Fund-raising efforts were proceeding when, in the spring of 2000, the state of Iowa established a new grant program entitled Vision Iowa. The program, initiated by Governor Vilsack and passed by the Iowa legislature, created a fund of $200 million for major programs across the state that would help reinvent the face of Iowa. The museum had been encouraged by leaders across the country to have the expansion interpret the entire Mississippi River, not just the Upper Mississippi. Creating a museum to encompass the entire Mississippi represented a substantial challenge; however, the museum believed that there was no other organization in the country capable of doing just that. Vision Iowa program funding would be critical if the museum were to pursue this new expansion.

After much deliberation and analysis, the museum applied for $20 million from Vision Iowa. If funded, the museum's expansion and endowment budget would grow from $25 million to $57 million. Vision Iowa funding would provide funds for the previously planned capital improvements as well as new improvements and would free up $4 million of donor funds which could be invested in endowment. Exhibit plans were reviewed and modified, and additional theaters, exhibits, and other features were added.

The museum had already completed an economic feasibility study which projected that the annual audience would be approximately 176,000 people a year. The revised expansion plans were reviewed by ConsultEcon, and a new visitor estimate was projected, showing a range of visitation of 230,000 to 309,000 people each year.[55] The pro-forma income and expense statement was also reviewed and updated. The museum was prepared to submit an application to Vision Iowa.

The city of Dubuque was also interested in securing Vision Iowa funds to build an education and conference center and make other infrastructure improvements. The city requested $38 million and with the museum jointly prepared an application in the amount of $58 million. The new project total was calculated at $188 million, which included the $58 million request as well as $130 million in matching funds. These matching funds showed substantial investment in infrastructure by the city as well as private investment as leveraged activity.[56]

Dubuque County had previously agreed to provide office space for the America's River campaign at the historic Old Jail, an 1857 National Historic Landmark, as well as $250,000 in cash support. At the request of the Vision Iowa board, Dubuque County contributed an additional $672,375 to bring their total investment to $1 million.[57]

In addition to cash contributions, America's River also received several donations of land, both outright transfers and long-term leases. The gifts of land from private sources totaled $6,038,500, not counting land made available by the city of Dubuque.[58]

The grant request consisted of hundreds of pages in four volumes, written over the course of four months by Enzler, with numerous reports and additions from team members. Twenty-five copies of the grant, weighing a total of 440 pounds, were submitted in December 2000.[59] On February 14, 2000, the America's River team made a one-hour presentation to the Vision Iowa board. The chair of the Vision Iowa board, Michael Gartner, told the team after the presentation, "There's not a person in this room that isn't just bowled over by your project." The Vision Iowa board voted to enter into negotiations with the city and the museum with a projected grant award of at least $30 million.[60] On April 12, 2001, the Vision Iowa board voted to award a total of $40 million to Dubuque, $20,000,081 to the museum, and $19,999,919 to the City of Dubuque.[61] This $40 million award was the first Vision Iowa grant award and represented 20 percent of the total funds available in the statewide program.

CONCLUSION

Ultimately, the entire America's River project was completed, including the museum's larger building, the additional exhibits, and the endowment. The goal had been to build a world-class museum that provided a place for people to explore the Mississippi River—past, present, and future. The museum achieved that goal and incorporated the most recent scholarship and partnered with numerous local, regional, and national agencies.[62] This growth had a tremendous effect on the museum[63] and on the community, including construction of the National Mississippi River Education and Conference Center, the Grand Harbor Resort and Indoor Water Park, and the Mississippi River Walk, Greenways, Amphitheater and other public amenities along with the associated infrastructure. The end result was a community and a region which has become engaged, excited, and aware of the enormous story of the Mississippi River and its watershed, not only its past but its future.[64]

NOTES

1. Jerry Enzler, "Application to Institute of Museum and Library Services for National Award for Museum and Library Service," 2005, Dubuque County Historical Society archives, with updated information added by author. Attendance at the Mississippi River Museum increased from 75,000 to 230,000 people annually, memberships increased from 480 to over 2,400 units, staff increased from 40 to 100 people, facilities increased from 29,000 to 88,000 square feet, outdoor interpretive space increased to 5 acres, and endowment increased from $600,000 to $4 million, all with no debt.

2. William Wilkie, *Dubuque on the Mississippi* (Dubuque: Loras College, 1990), 129.

3. William Wilkie, *Dubuque on the Mississippi* (Dubuque: Loras College, 1990), 143–477.

4. US Census, 2000. Dubuque County population in 2000 was 89,156.

5. "Articles of Incorporation," Dubuque County Historical Society, 1950, 1.

6. Dubuque County Historical Society archives.

7. Artifact accession records, 1965, Dubuque County Historical Society archives.

8. Treasurer's Report, December 31, 1977, Dubuque County Historical Society archives.

9. Treasurer's Report, December 31, 1992, Dubuque County Historical Society archives.

10. *Telegraph Herald*, August 13, 1995, A1.

11. Jerry Enzler and Roger Osborne, *Launchings: Dubuque Boats and Boat Builders* (Dubuque: Dubuque County Historical Society, 1985).

12. Wayne A. Norman Sr., *National Endowment for the Humanities Self Study Grant,* 1975, Dubuque County Historical Society archives.

13. December 1978, Dubuque County Historical Society archives.

14. March 1979, Dubuque County Historical Society archives.

15. Fund drive records, 1979 to 1980, Dubuque County Historical Society archives.

16. "Steaming into the Port of Dubuque Fund Drive Records, 1983–1986," Dubuque County Historical Society archives.

17. Minutes of Meeting of the Board of Directors, 1984, Dubuque County Historical Society archives.

18. Minutes of the Board of Directors, 1986, Dubuque County Historical Society archives.

19. "Make the Dream a Reality" fund drive records and NEH challenge grant document, 1990, Dubuque County Historical Society archives.

20. Informal Survey of Visitors, 1992, Dubuque County Historical Society archives.

21. Long Range Planning Minutes, 1992, Dubuque County Historical Society archives.

22. Minutes of Board of Directors, 1992, Dubuque County Historical Society archives.

23. Jerry Enzler records, Dubuque County Historical Society archives.

24. Jerry Enzler, Lyons/Zaremba, *River Discovery Center Interpretive Plan*, Dubuque County Historical Society archives.

25. William Woodward and Jerry Enzler, "Vision 2000," Dubuque County Historical Society annual meeting minutes, January 1995, Dubuque County Historical Society archives.

26. John Walsh was vice president of mortgage lending at Dubuque Bank and Trust and then president of the society most of the time that the museum and aquarium was being built. Wayne A. Norman Sr. was believed by many to be the most energetic and accomplished volunteer civic leader in the community, having successfully completed more than a dozen educational, cultural, and religious projects. (See Telegraph Herald 1st Citizen Award and Dubuque County Historical Society Treasures of Dubuque Award in Norman File, Dubuque County Historical Society archives.) Tim Conlon, Conlon Construction Company, ultimately resigned so that he could bid without con-

flict of interest for the job of construction manager for the project. His firm successfully coordinated the work of over fifty contractors, winning the Iowa Master Builders award for their work. Jeff Bertsch, senior vice president of Flexsteel, was serving as treasurer of the society and kept an eye on the expenditures. Paul Woodward, the oldest son of the lead donor, Bill Woodward, brought a business management approach and attention to follow-through to the planning process. Jim Gantz, president of Lime Rock Springs Bottling Company, local bottler for Pepsi, joined the building committee when he became an officer of the Dubuque County Historical Society. Milt Avenarius was retired from Paulson Electric Company and had significant experience in construction and contractor relations.

27. Jerry Enzler and Lyons/Zaremba, *River Discovery Center Interpretive Plan*, Dubuque County Historical Society archives.

28. Fund-raising agreement between chamber and society, 1997, Dubuque County Historical Society archives.

29. *America's River Case Statement*, Dubuque County Historical Society archives.

30. $1.86 million from William Woodward, $1 million from the state of Iowa, over $600,000 from the National Endowment for the Humanities, $496,000 from a recent local bequest from a donor named Helen Everest, and funds the city was willing to invest towards the river walk.

31. Howard Braren Associates, Inc., *America's River Fund Raising Feasibility Study*, Dubuque County Historical Society archives.

32. Jerry Enzler, *America's River Vision Iowa Application*, 2000, Iowa Department of Economic Development, Dubuque County Historical Society archives.

33. "River Project Nets $1 Million Donation," *Telegraph Herald*, September 13, 1998.

34. The professor's class developed a media plan that included miniature aquarium tanks that contained press releases.

35. Activities and festivals included a walkathon, six jazz fests, Swing Fest, the annual Taste of Dubuque festival, which drew over ten thousand people, the Dubuque County Fair, Riverfest, Dubuque Fest, and the annual Chili Cook Off. Volunteers at these festivals donated over five thousand hours, wearing T-shirts and stickers identifying America's River.

36. The *Dubuque Telegraph Herald* donated an eight-page, ad-free insert, which was delivered with each newspaper, and printed an overrun of ten thousand copies for mailing and face-to-face distribution. Lamar Outdoor Advertising donated an oversized billboard with the campaign logo and slogan for six months. Television stations KFXB Dubuque, the Fox affiliate, and KWWL Waterloo, the NBC affiliate, donated airtime for the campaign commercial. Eight tristate radio stations donated a six-month schedule of public service announcements, valued at $30,000. America's River was publicized through regular features in the City of Dubuque's *City Focus*, a print newsletter which was sent to every home in the city quarterly. A half-hour video interview about America's River was replayed on the city channel 8 government access station on cable television each month for over two years. In addition, campaign officials secured regular coverage in the *Telegraph Herald* daily newspaper and *Julien's Journal* monthly magazine.

37. A Clarke College honors class researched topics, including point-source pollution, water quality, effects of engineering the river, and the current state of habitat and wildlife, and reported their findings to the director. Northeast Iowa Community College hosted a planning session for the museum and the education and conference center. Iowa State University Extension agreed to provide ongoing partial funding of one of the key museum staff positions. The University of Iowa's Hydrology Department collaborated on exhibit development. Tulane University consulted on research and planning.

38. Working with the Catfish Creek Coalition, the River Discovery Consortium coordinated a storm drain stenciling initiative. This was a major volunteer effort in the community to actively involve its citizens in raising awareness about river conservation. Over 200 volunteers, including many high school and grade school students,

were recruited to apply a stencil message, "Dump no waste, drains to river," to 1,400 drains that are part of the city's storm water removal system. Outreach included public access television programming, classroom visits by the consortium coordinator, and brochures explaining the effort distributed door to door in neighborhoods where the stenciling was done.

39. As of 2006, the network had grown to 62 museums and featured a sign in front of most of the museums, 100,000 copies of an interpretive brochure, and plans for a major traveling exhibit.

40. Presentations and appearances included speaking opportunities at the National Waterways Conference, the Gulf Intracoastal Waterways Association, Mississippi River Summits, Midwest Area River Coalition, the Army Corps of Engineers Partnering Conference, and the Environmental Grant Makers Annual Retreat.

41. These leaders included Vernon Behrhorst, former director of Gulf Intracoastal Waterways Association; Chris Brescia, President, Midwest Area River Coalition 2000, St. Louis; Harry Cook, President, National Waterways Conference; Michael Hagan, President and CEO, American Commercial Lines, the world's largest barge line at the time; Berdon Lawrence, President and CEO, Kirby Corporation; Fred Luckey, Vice President, Bunge Corporation, St. Louis; J. Merrick Jones, President, Canal Barge Company, New Orleans; Terry Becker, President, Riverway Barge Company, Minneapolis; Captain Bill Bowell, owner of the Padelford Packet Company Excursion Boats in St. Paul, Minnesota; Robert and Ruth Kehl, winners of the US Small Business Persons of the Year for 1986; John Hartford, a three-time Grammy-award-winning river musician of Nashville, Tennessee; and former Iowa governor Terry Branstad, who traveled to New Orleans on behalf of the project to host a reception for the inland waterways shipping industry and agribusiness.

42. Gift agreement between Captain William Bowell and Society, Dubuque County Historical Society archives.

43. US Fish and Wildlife Service Agreement, Dubuque County Historical Society archives.

44. US Army Corps of Engineers Agreement, Dubuque County Historical Society archives.

45. US Coast Guard Agreement, Dubuque County Historical Society archives.

46. Smithsonian Affiliate Agreement, Dubuque County Historical Society archives.

47. "Federal Official Falls under Mississippi's Spell," *Telegraph Herald*, July 31, 1998.

48. The task force included Congressmen Jim Nussle, Jim Leach, Leonard Boswell, and Tom Latham of Iowa; Ron Kind of Wisconsin; Gil Gutnecht and James Oberstar of Minnesota; Lane Evans of Illinois; and Bennie Thompson of Mississippi.

49. Upper Mississippi River Congressional Task Force, April 5, 1999.

50. "Dubuquers Make Pitch for Center to Congress," *Telegraph Herald*, April 16, 1999.

51. Testimony of Jerry Enzler to US House of Representatives Appropriations Subcommittee on Interior and Related Agencies, March 3, 1998, Dubuque County Historical Society archives.

52. William R. Ferris, Chairman, National Endowment for the Humanities, February 15, 2000, Dubuque County Historical Society archives.

53. Letter from five governors to US Congress, April 28, 1999, fund drive records, Dubuque County Historical Society archives. The letter was signed by Governor Tom Vilsack, Iowa; Governor George Ryan, Illinois; Governor Tommy Thompson, Wisconsin; Governor Jesse Ventura, Minnesota; and Governor Mel Carnahan, Missouri, and dated April 28, 1999.

54. $3.2 million was secured in two appropriations from Labor and Health and Human Services by Senator Harkin for exhibits for the museum. $800,000 was secured by Senator Harkin from US Department of Housing and Urban Development (HUD) for planning and design. Six different National Scenic Byway or Transportation enhancement grants were secured through the competitive grant process, $629,630, $444,050, $329,920, $322,760, $170,400, and $169,323. Five grants were secured from the

62 Jerome Enzler

National Endowment for the Humanities: a $500,000 challenge grant; a $300,530 exhibit grant; a $150,000 exhibit grant; a $51,081 planning grant; and a $20,000 self-study grant. A National Park Service Grant of $25,500 helped provide funds for the outdoor boatyard exhibit development to tell the story of the boat building industry which took place on the site for over a hundred years.

55. ConsultEcon, "Economic Feasibility Studies for the Mississippi River Museum," Dubuque County Historical Society archives.

56. Jerry Enzler, *America's River Vision Iowa Application*, 2000, Iowa Department of Economic Development, Dubuque County Historical Society archives. A local hotel developer, Platinum Holdings, LLC, committed to a first-phase investment of $21,500,000 for a riverfront hotel with approximately 200 rooms, which features an enclosed water park of 24,000 square feet. Platinum Holdings, LLC also contingently committed to a second-phase investment of $16 million to add approximately 150 additional rooms and another 18,000 square feet to the water park. Durrant Group, a national architectural and engineering firm headquartered in Dubuque, also committed to the construction of an office building as part of the campus at $5.5 million.

57. "County Boosts Contributions to America's River Project," *Telegraph Herald*, April 10, 2001.

58. Jerry Enzler, *America's River Vision Iowa Application*, 2000, Iowa Department of Economic Development.

59. "440 Pounds Worth of Proposals," *Telegraph Herald*, December 21, 2000.

60. "Vision Iowa Offers $30 Million," *Telegraph Herald*, February 14, 2001.

61. "Vision Iowa Grant Totals $40 Million," *Telegraph Herald*, April 12, 2003; Vision Iowa Contract, Dubuque County Historical Society archives.

62. "A Dream Realized," *Telegraph Herald*, June 28, 2003.

63. Treasurer's Reports and Board Minutes, 2004, 2005, 2006, Dubuque County Historical Society archives. The museum audience increased from 70,000 to 230,000 annually. Museum memberships increased from 680 to 2,000 while membership income increased from $60,000 to $240,000 annually. Revenues increased from $100,000 to $1.5 million, the annual budget increased from $750,000 to $4.2 million, and the endowment grew from $600,000 to $4 million. Staff also grew from thirteen full-time to thirty-three full-time employees and from forty part-time to sixty-seven part-time employees. The museum became a major center of environmental learning and historic appreciation of the Mississippi River.

64. Bob Byrne, "Myrtle the Turtle Will Help Change Dubuque: New River Museum Is a Huge Triumph for City's Visionaries," *Telegraph Herald*, July 14, 2003.

BIBLIOGRAPHY

"440 Pounds Worth of Proposals." *Telegraph Herald*, December 21, 2000.
"A Dream Realized." *Telegraph Herald*, June 28, 2003.
Byrne, Bob. "Myrtle the Turtle Will Help Change Dubuque: New River Museum Is a Huge Triumph for City's Visionaries." *Telegraph Herald*, July 14, 2003.
Clarke College commencement, May 2001.
"County Boosts Contributions to America's River Project." *Telegraph Herald*, April 10, 2001.
"Dubuquers Make Pitch for Center to Congress." *Telegraph Herald*, April 16, 1999.
Enzler, Jerry, and Roger Osborne. *Launchings: Dubuque Boats and Boat Builders*. Dubuque, IA: Dubuque County Historical Society, 1985.
"Federal Official Falls under Mississippi's Spell." *Telegraph Herald*, July 31, 1998.
"Jaycees Step Up for Heritage Trail-Blazing." *Telegraph Herald*, May 3, 2000.
Loras College commencement, May 2006.
Lyons/Zaremba, ConsultEcon, Jerry Enzler, et al. *Mississippi River Museum Expansion Study*. February 2005.
"Project Leaders Celebrate Grant." *Telegraph Herald*, April 13, 2001.

"River Project Nets $1 Million Donation." *Telegraph Herald,* September 13, 1998.
Scarpino, Philip. *Great River: An Environmental History of the Upper Mississippi, 1890–1950.* Columbia: University of Missouri Press.
State of Iowa, Office of the Governor and Lieutenant Governor. August 9, 2006. www.governor.state.ia.us/news/2006/august/august0906.
Telegraph Herald, August 13, 1995.
Upper Mississippi River Congressional Task Force, April 5, 1999.
US Census, 2000.
Vision Iowa board meeting minutes. Iowa Department of Economic Development, December 13, 2006.
"Vision Iowa Grant Totals $40 Million." *Telegraph Herald,* April 12, 2003.
"Vision Iowa Offers $30 Million." *Telegraph Herald,* February 14, 2001.
Wilkie, William. *Dubuque on the Mississippi.* Dubuque, IA: Loras College, 1990.

Dubuque County Historical Society Archives

America's River Case Statement.
Articles of Incorporation, 1950.
Artifact accession records.
Board Minutes, 1977–2006.
Cawley, Ed. Theme Study for River Discovery Center.
ConsultEcon. Economic Feasibility Studies for the Mississippi River Museum.
Enzler, Jerry. *America's River Vision Iowa Application,* Iowa Department of Economic Development, 2000.
———. "Application to Institute of Museum and Library Services for National Award for Museum and Library Service," 2005.
———. *Mississippi River Museum & Aquarium Vision Iowa Application,* October 1, 2006.
———. National Endowment for the Humanities challenge grant application, 1999.
———. Records.
———. Testimony to US House of Representatives Appropriations Subcommittee on Interior and Related Agencies, March 3, 1998.
Enzler, Jerry, and Lyons/Zaremba. *River Discovery Center Interpretive Plan.*
Ferris, William. Chairman, National Endowment for the Humanities, February 15, 2000.
Fund drive records, 1979 to 1980.
Fund-raising agreement between chamber and society, 1977.
Gift agreement between Captain William Bowell and Society.
Hawes, Edward, et al. *River Discovery Center Interpretive Master Plan.*
Howard Braren Associates, Inc. *America's River Fund Raising Feasibility Study.*
Informal Survey of Visitors, 1992.
Iowa Community Attraction and Tourism Development contract.
Letter from five governors to US Congress, April 28, 1999.
Long Range Planning Minutes, 1992.
Make the Dream a Reality fund drive records.
NEH challenge grant document, 1990.
Norman, Wayne A., Sr. *National Endowment for the Humanities Self Study Grant,* 1975.
Senator John C. Culver. Letter, March 10, 1999.
Smithsonian Affiliate Agreement.
Steaming into the Port of Dubuque fund drive records, 1983–1986.
Treasurer's reports, 1977–2006.
US Army Corps of Engineers Agreement.
US Coast Guard Agreement.
US Fish and Wildlife Service Agreement.
Vernon Research Group. Survey of National Mississippi River Museum & Aquarium Visitors, 2005.
Vision Iowa contract, 2001.

Woodward, William, and Jerry Enzler. "Vision 2000."

FIVE

The Great Transformation at the Strong

Amy Hollister Zarlengo

The Strong, located in Rochester, New York, had its beginning in Margaret Woodbury Strong's desire to see her collection of 300,000 objects, her "fascinations," displayed in a museum for the education and enjoyment of the public. The case details the Strong's entrepreneurial journey from a struggling decorative arts museum with no articulated vision and poor attendance to a museum of national caliber focused on the cultural history of play serving over half a million visitors a year. The Strong's journey is marked by decades of diligent strategic planning influenced by market research. The result was the creation of a flexible business culture and responsive operational structure that promoted innovation and creativity and allowed the institution to identify community needs and capitalize on opportunities. Today, with expanded audiences including families and scholars locally, nationally, and internationally, community collaborations, and innovative programs that serve the public, the Strong is a relevant institution of national caliber.

INTRODUCTION

Margaret Woodbury Strong (1897–1969) was the only child of John Woodbury, an investor in the Eastman Kodak Company. The family's wealth provided both social status and opportunities that shaped Margaret's life. As a child, her family traveled frequently, visited museums, and attended theater productions. The family travels and lifestyle prevented Margaret from completing a formal education, instead learning from tu-

Figure 5.1. Exterior of The Strong in Rochester, New York. *Courtesy The Strong, Rochester, N.Y.*

tors and adults in her extended family.[1] Her lifestyle of continuous informal education contributed to her desire to share her collections and drove her to create her museum.

Margaret's personal collecting began on family trips as a child. She rarely wrote about the motives that governed her collecting, but on a tour, museum visitors can learn that Margaret started collecting miniatures because her parents allowed her to purchase anything that could fit in one bag, and she could fit more if she sought out smaller objects.[2] In 1920, Margaret married Homer Strong, and they had a child, Barbara, in 1921. Barbara died in 1945 at the age of twenty-four, and Homer died twelve years later, in 1957. After her husband's death, Margaret's collection grew rapidly. She collected broadly and with considerable depth, although she was best known for her dolls and toys, of which she had over 27,000 by the mid-1960s.[3]

During the late 1950s and 1960s, Margaret began to think of her collection as a museum. She added 20,000 square feet to her 25,000-square-foot house to display her objects and conduct tours. She also obtained a provisional charter for her "Museum of Fascination" from the New York State Board of Regents in 1968 with a stated mission "to preserve, protect, restore, and exhibit objects and properties of unusual interest from the past and present for the edification and enjoyment of the public."[4] At the time of her death in 1969, Margaret's collections or "fascinations" included more than 17,000 dolls, 400 dollhouses, 4,000 toys, 2,000 paintings, 12,000 prints, 900 costumes, 100 quilts and coverlets, 600 paperweights, 7,500 glass objects, 1,350 pieces of furniture, and more.[5] Very few of the 300,000 objects had any documentation.

Margaret's will dictated the provisions for establishing the Margaret Woodbury Strong Museum of Fascination. She left the majority of her estate to the museum corporation, including her property, finances, and collections, and gave her executors the discretion to determine what portion of her estate would be needed to staff and maintain the museum.[6] Margaret also instructed the board of trustees to determine whether a museum could be made from her collection, and if so, to use as much of her estate as necessary and distribute the remainder to selected organizations, a determination to be made within three years of her death.[7] Most importantly, she gave the trustees and executors of her will the discretion to determine which parts of her collection were appropriate for a museum, which granted them permission to shape the collection to best serve the public need.

The first board of trustees, led by Thomas E. McFarland, included nine members, all of whom were professional or community leaders in Rochester, and the executors of the estate and the attorney who drew Margaret Strong's will.[8] This group, not yet familiar with the museum profession, inherited numerous challenges. To justify keeping her estate, which was valued at $54 million, instead of distributing it to nineteen charities and social services, the new museum had to provide a worthwhile educational experience.

THE BIRTH OF A PROFESSIONAL INSTITUTION, 1969–1987

Faced with the challenge of realizing the true educational value of Margaret Strong's collection, the board of trustees cautiously established the Margaret Woodbury Strong Museum in 1971 and called upon Holman J. Swinney, director of the Adirondack Museum, to consult on the scope of the collection and make recommendations for the museum. Swinney advised the trustees on how to make the transition from a personal collection to a viable, educational museum. He recognized that the museum's extensive collection was its biggest asset and obstacle; without a well-interpreted collection, a museum was an ineffective educational tool. Unless the board of trustees committed to a transition from personal collection to a focused, educational institution with a larger purpose, the museum would fail.[9] Swinney believed "a museum's building is a housing for the collections and staff—and for the educational program which is the only reasonable rationale for the existence of so complex and costly an institution as a museum."[10] The trustees hired Swinney as their first director in 1972.

Swinney hired fifteen staff members to help manage the collections and to plan for and secure the new museum and brought in five museum leaders to consult on possible interpretive themes. All five agreed the common thread running throughout the collection was that every object delighted Margaret Strong. Almost all mentioned the potential for a museum focused on play or fantasy, but none recommended it. The consultants did agree that the Margaret Woodbury Strong Museum should be planned as a model institution, and E. McClung Fleming, head of the Winterthur Museum's education department, recommended creating a museum of Victorian culture, Victorian popular culture, or taste and fashion.[11]

Swinney and the trustees agreed the Strong Museum would interpret the "popular social and cultural development of Northeastern America in the post-industrial period." The majority of the collection was from the nineteenth and early twentieth centuries, representing objects of mass production more frequently than individual craftsmanship, a theme interpreted by few other museums.[12] Due to the size of the collection, Swinney proposed creating an electronic cataloguing system and dedicating a portion of gallery space to open storage in order to make more of the expansive collection visible to visitors. These innovations contributed greatly to the Margaret Woodbury Strong Museum's professional reputation.

With the question of how to interpret the collection resolved, the board of trustees settled Margaret Strong's estate, which had grown to $77 million by 1973.[13] The trustees then turned their full attention to building a new facility on Margaret Strong's property. However, neighborhood protests in the fall of 1976, bolstered by the threat of legal intervention that would have delayed construction by three years, led the trustees to purchase property in downtown Rochester in 1979.[14] On June 1, 1979, the museum broke ground on a 160,000-square-foot building on 13.5 acres of land in downtown Rochester, ultimately costing $12.5 million.[15]

As Swinney worked to build the institution, the staff worked to get the collection under control. In 1978, with a grant from the Smithsonian's National Museum Act, Robert Chenhall, Director of Data Services, published *Nomenclature for Museum Cataloging: A System for Classifying Man-Made Objects*. The book was Swinney's brainchild, and the project contributed greatly to the profession's excitement at the museum's opening.

In July of 1981, Swinney announced his intention to retire at the opening of the facility and the national search for a new director began. In July 1982, the Margaret Woodbury Strong Museum ranked among the top fifteen most desirable director positions in the country. The trustees eventually selected Swinney's long-time friend, William T. Alderson, who led Tennessee State Library and Archives, American Association for State and Local History, and the Museum Studies Program at the University of Delaware.

After eleven years of planning and with the support of eighty-one full-time employees and one hundred volunteers, the Margaret Woodbury Strong Museum opened on October 12, 1982. The fully handicapped-accessible building contained 33,000 square feet of exhibition space; 18,000 square feet of open storage; 2,800 square feet of classroom/workspace; a library; and a 290-seat auditorium.[16] At the opening reception, museum professionals were impressed and intrigued by Swinney's open storage, which consisted of 315 exhibit cases filled with 19,000 objects.[17] The following spring, the museum won multiple professional awards.

With the museum open, the board of trustees sought a permanent charter from the New York State Board of Regents and applied for and received accreditation through the American Alliance of Museums (AAM). The first year was successful; the 1983 budget was $3.379 million, 84 percent of which was funded through endowment income.[18] In 1982, during less than three months of operation, over fifty thousand people visited the museum, fulfilling attendance levels anticipated by the trustees. Between October 1983 and October 1984, 143,800 visitors came through the doors.[19]

By September 1983, however, the trustees began to worry about monthly attendance. Program attendance was high, but daily attendance was low. The chairman of the board suggested the museum begin strategic planning, but Alderson argued that any planning "sooner than the end of the second or third year of operation [would] be a meaningless exercise in speculation."[20] Instead, Alderson completed a ten-year projection which included program options and financial recommendations focused on maintaining the scholarly reputation of the Margaret Woodbury Strong Museum.

By August of 1984, decreasing attendance was a serious focus for the board of trustees. The decrease was dramatic; January–July 1983 attendance was 93,000 people, yet the same period in 1984 showed a decrease of 35,000 visitors.[21] Trustees reexamined exhibits, programs, and public relations; solicited visitor feedback through exit interviews; and joined a telephone survey with four other local institutions. Analysis of the results revealed that the museum appealed more to white-collar adults and to those with higher education and an appreciation for history.[22]

In examining the museum's programs and audience, Alderson and staff realized the statement of purpose needed greater clarity. The new statement incorporated Margaret's original statement of purpose for her museum of fascination and more accurately reflected the museum's exhibits and programs by focusing the interpretation on the lifestyles of ordinary Americans.

In 1984, Alderson proposed that the trustees develop a committee of visitors, external museum leaders who would serve a three-year term, visiting once per year to perform an evaluation and make recommendations.[23] The committee addressed the issue of declining attendance and recommended that the institution focus locally, something seriously considered by the trustees in the years to come.[24] Warren Leon, director of interpretation at Old Sturbridge Village, attributed the Strong Museum's low attendance to exhibit content, approach, and the museum's public image. Based on conversations with Rochester residents, Leon noted that because of Margaret Strong's reputation, visitors expected a museum about the eccentric founder's life or dolls, not "significant insights into American history," and that the Strong Museum made "concepts of fun and education seem antithetical."[25]

Over the next year, the museum started many initiatives and planning committees designed to address the issue of declining attendance. The newly opened Tuckaway Café, an onsite restaurant, was intended to increase visit time. Once again, attendance at programs was high, while daily visitation remained low.[26] In 1985, a subtle shift in exhibition themes began. While previous exhibits focused on the decorative arts (household furnishings, historic toys, and the arts and crafts movement), the museum began to incorporate exhibits that appealed to broader audiences (American entertainment and fitness). Even with these changes, there were few opportunities for audience participation in interactive experiences outside of exchanges with a docent. Attendance for 1985 was 69,498—less than half that of 1983.[27] In October 1986, William T. Alderson resigned.

In addition to the resignation of Alderson, two other important transitions took place in 1986: the use of exhibition teams and the creation of *One History Place*. Inspired by a Kellogg Foundation workshop, the Strong Museum began using exhibition teams consisting of a historian, curator, designer, and educator to plan upcoming exhibits.[28] These teams would eventually become the basis for creating a flexible, boundaryless organizational structure. One of these teams began planning *One History Place*, the Strong Museum's first interactive exhibit.

One History Place was inspired by the results of a survey conducted by the community action group the Junior League in January 1986. Results indicated that 96.7 percent of respondents desired a museum with "hands-on experience for young children" ages three through third grade.[29] The Strong Museum's education staff had acknowledged that there was a programming gap and that the museum did not serve young children. The survey gave the education staff the push they needed and helped them recognize that programs for young children would be well attended.[30] The Strong Museum, supported by Junior League funding and volunteers, began to plan for *One History Place* through benchmarking children's museums, observing early childhood classes, and studying developmental educational theories.[31] An exhibit team developed *One History Place* through formative evaluation techniques and tested the exhibit with over seven hundred children.[32] These evaluation techniques helped the team create exhibit content and design that encouraged thinking skills strategies in visitors, determined whether the exhibit met learning objectives, and tested interactives.[33]

One History Place, which opened in 1987, dramatically boosted attendance. Children could "play with stuffed animals, blocks and storybooks in an 1890s parlor or experiment with 80-year-old utensils in a mock-up of a Victorian kitchen, or sneak into a recreated attic where they can dig into a large steamer trunk to play dress up with period clothing."[34] *One History Place*'s successful community engagement quickly became a mandate for the new director, G. Rollie Adams, who started just three weeks prior to its opening.

THE TRANSFORMATIVE YEARS, 1987–2006

The trustees remained concerned with declining attendance, having closed William Alderson's last year as director in 1986 at 76,353 visitors, a 9.9 percent increase from the previous year, but still well below attendance goals.[35] In the executive director search, the trustees identified two major tasks: to make the Strong Museum critically important in the community and to begin strategic planning. In September 1987, G. Rollie Adams joined the Strong Museum as president and chief executive officer and immediately set about effecting change at the institution. Adams inherited an institution that had successfully embraced professional standards but had failed to provide content relevant to and engaging for a general audience. In setting goals for the organization, Adams wanted to maintain the "standard-setting program of collections care and management" and operate "in accordance with the highest professional museum and business standards."[36] He also recognized areas of opportunity and had come to the Strong Museum because he understood the institution had unrealized potential and the resources to make a difference.[37] Adams, senior staff, and the trustees immediately began to assess these opportunities through strategic planning. Under Adams's leadership, the Strong Museum would undergo five separate strategic planning efforts in 1989, 1994, 1999, 2004, and 2008. Each time, the board of trustees approved a two-year plan and extended the plan annually until completed, at which point they developed another plan.[38] Each strategic plan drove changes and was crafted in the context of the changes driven by the previous plan.

1989–1993: Laying the Groundwork for Change

Events stemming from the 1989 strategic plan prepared the institution, which had changed little since opening, for the dramatic transformation that lay ahead. The long-range planning committee, facilitated by the Winters Group, a consulting firm, first met in January 1988 to develop a planning method. The committee determined that the planning process would include goals and action steps and be "evergreen," a term brought to the institution by the trustees, meaning that the institution would review the progress toward strategic plan goals annually and, if needed, edit or drop them.

The 1989 strategic plan was very broad. The Winters Group's surveys of board, staff, volunteers, area educators, and the community revealed that the museum's board of trustees and museum staff had different ideas of how to make the museum critical to the community and advance the institution.[39] As a result, the first strategic plan promoted exploration of different projects and ideas, including everything from starting a popular magazine (never realized) to writing a scholarly journal (tabled for twenty years).[40] The plan also began the conversation about institutional vision and produced the first articulated vision statement: "The Strong Museum is the leading history museum in the country. It provides the highest quality service to the public through its superb collections and through educational programs that are innovative, interactive, imaginative, and entertaining."[41]

As the museum conducted market research and increased the interactivity of the programs, and as the community responded with increased attendance, the board and staff reviewed and changed the mission accordingly. Mission changes made while developing the 1989 strategic plan were minimal. The 1984 mission stated "the collections are used to advance the understanding . . . of ordinary Americans," which the museum presented in traditional decorative arts–style exhibitions. The 1989 mission, while similar to the 1984 mission, added the critical phrase "tell the story of everyday life in America." In telling the story of everyday life, the museum began to shift focus from decorative arts to social history.

To more effectively market this shift, the institution developed the tagline "Exploring American Life." Exhibits in 1988 and 1989 featured Victorian parlors, but in 1990 the institution shifted focus slightly to include class perspective, highlighting American advertising and ice cream's transition from elite food to one for all classes. In 1990, the museum again reviewed its mission statement and found that as the museum incorporated more social history themes, the mission's stated 1940 end date was too restrictive. By ending the museum's historic interpretation at 1940, the museum would soon be unable to use living memory as an educational tool to connect with visitors.[42] As a result, the Strong

Museum expanded its interpretation into the second half of the twentieth century.

Exhibits in 1991 moved further away from the decorative arts focus by examining the radio in American life and the American middle class. Finally, in 1992, the museum fully committed the collections to interpreting social history themes relevant to modern American life and opened *Altered States: Alcohol and Other Drugs in America*, followed by *Memories and Mourning: American Expressions of Grief* in 1993. Most exhibitions had community advisory committees, and social service groups were invited to "treat exhibits as a stage or platform in which to offer community programs to serve their audiences and missions."[43] The Strong Museum also designed collaborative programs to accompany these exhibits, including alcohol and drug lessons for Rochester fifth- and sixth-graders and public conferences on bereavement and grief counseling.[44] Through these collaborations, the museum's service to and connection with the community strengthened. The focus on social history and the resounding success of *One History Place* drove attendance from 107,747 in 1988 to 132,408 in 1993, peaking at 135,701 in 1991.[45] During years of overall low visitation, program attendance was high, but new programs, especially Tuesdays for Tots, a program that provided live entertainment for toddlers, attracted young audiences and families like never before.[46] It was becoming clear that the community wanted children's activities and that incorporating these activities into programming represented a key opportunity for the Strong Museum to engage the community.

In 1992, the Strong Museum undertook its first serious study to analyze the potential of programming for children. The market survey of Monroe County, conducted by the Winters Group, identified children's activities of high interest to the community and assessed the potential of the children's market. Results indicated that while attendance had increased and the community was more involved at the museum, public perception of the institution was divided; 44 percent of respondents viewed the Strong Museum as a doll museum (an image the decorative arts and now social history institution had been trying to discourage from its opening), while 37 percent viewed it as a history museum.[47] Finally, the survey revealed that in 1991, the Strong Museum served 20 percent of the regional family market and through expanded family exhibits and programs with low admission had the potential to double its reach.[48]

The Strong Museum was highly motivated to expand the organization's capacity by capitalizing on research results to increase attendance and community engagement. However, the institution also wanted to ensure the collection could support the mission and educational approach, which led to detailed internal research regarding the feasibility of expanding children's programming. This report called for the creation of a "special ad hoc board-staff team to develop a plan to meet long-term facilities' needs."[49]

1994–1998: Developing a Shared Vision

One major success of the 1994 strategic plan was the development of a shared vision. This was critical because implementation of the 1994 strategic plan and extensions brought about widespread institutional change, from operations to mission and vision. The Strong Museum successfully applied for multiple Institute of Museum Services grants (IMS, now the Institute of Museum and Library Services), competitive grants that were attainable because of the professional reputation developed during Swinney and Alderson's tenure and that continued through Adams's tenure. The grants funded market research, consultants, and traveling to benchmark model sites with successful children's programs. Staff and trustees visited model institutions and looked at everything from the facility to exhibits and programs to determine what would work with the Strong Museum's new family-centric direction.

In 1994, the Strong Museum launched another market study, this one including a geodemographic survey that profiled the market by zip code over a larger radius (sixty-five miles) and focus groups, to determine "motivators and barriers, perceptions and attitudes which affect museum participation and the overall marketing plan for the museum."[50] The results reinforced the findings from the 1992 market survey that with aggressive marketing the museum could nearly double current attendance and increase membership another 40 percent within three to five years by providing programs for children.[51] In order to do so, the Strong Museum needed to communicate to its audience "clear name recognition, clear understanding of what to expect, [and] a knowledge that the museum is not stuffy and dusty with old exhibits."[52]

Updated mission and vision statements better reflected the growing relationship between the institution and the community. The 1993 mission demonstrated a stronger commitment to social history and to the community by aiming to "help people in and beyond Greater Rochester understand the past and plan the future."[53] The Strong Museum reaffirmed its commitment to social history a year later with the mission, "exploring progress, class, and identity in order to help people better understand themselves and each other, individually and collectively." To carry out the mission, the Strong Museum took the same collection used for decorative arts exhibits and asked different types of questions to make exhibits relevant to broader audiences and increasingly more beneficial to the community.[54]

These mission and vision statements, aided by the interpretive themes of class, progress, and identity, did a better job than their predecessors at defining the institution's purpose by effectively communicating the institution's identity as a social history institution with family appeal, a substantial transition from the decorative arts institution of the 1980s. In January 1995, brainstorming exercises with staff and trustees revealed convergent thinking on the new direction, particularly as it related to an emphasis on families.[55]

From benchmarking other institutions, the Strong Museum determined future exhibitions would be more dynamic and compelling, more interactive for all ages, more experiential, and larger in scale and that they would incorporate learning opportunities in a variety of levels and styles.[56] The new approach was launched in 1994 and included *When Barbie Dated G.I. Joe*. The 1995 exhibit, *Small Wonders: A Fantastic Voyage into the Miniature World*, incorporated higher levels of interactivity, and *Kid to Kid* examined how children communicate with each other. The interpretive focus had shifted from exhibits that identified "a historical problem and solved it in a way that contributes to contemporary discourse" to exhibits that demonstrated "education will entertain us; that our country is rightfully and routinely multicultural; that women and men are equal; that children can learn despite disadvantage; that early education is crucial; and that kids can learn about hard subjects."[57]

The ad hoc facilities planning team concluded that the building would have to be expanded to meet exhibition, increased programming, and collection storage goals. This also provided an opportunity to address visitation barriers respondents identified in the 1994 market study: the distance between the entrance and parking and food service.[58] In 1997, the Strong Museum opened a new 12,000-square-foot atrium entrance adjacent to the parking lot that included a 1950s diner and 1918 carousel. At the same time, the museum opened *Wegman's Super Kids Market* and *Can You Tell Me How to Get to Sesame Street?*, a collaboration with the Children's Television Workshop. To communicate these changes, the Strong Museum rebranded as "the Fun History Place for Kids of All Ages." With the opening of the new atrium, new interactive exhibits, and marketing, attendance growth, which had leveled off between 1991 and 1994, increased from 142,555 in 1995 to 234,671 in 1997 and surpassed 300,000 in the following year.[59] Memberships increased from 2,538 units to 7,160 units in two years.[60]

The 1994 strategic plan also included strategies to implement total quality management (TQM), a management philosophy under which everyone in the organization holds responsibility for continuously improving products and processes. Senior management completed training courses focused on effective and efficient techniques for brainstorming, running meetings, and eliciting more participation.[61]

In April 1994, the trustees solicited the services of a quality trainer from Xerox to coordinate customer service and help roll out TQM.[62] Staff members were not receptive to the training. Trustees formally halted TQM implementation and asked senior staff to demonstrate the techniques and behaviors and to lead the institutional philosophy by example.[63] While formally adopting TQM was unsuccessful, the institution gained powerful tools that greatly increased its ability to respond to opportunities.

Experimentation with total quality management planted the seed for the guest services program and encouraged the development of a new institutional operation philosophy called boundaryless organization structure.[64] Alderson's exhibit team concept from the 1980s, when coupled with total quality management's emphasis on teamwork, led to a desire for a completely team-oriented institution.[65]

Fueled by communication and meeting management techniques learned from the TQM attempt, the museum slowly changed its organizational structure. In 1994, the word "group" was substituted for division and additional cross-function teams were created, including one to study communication practices at the institution.[66] Five years later, the Strong Museum increased staff training and soon after eliminated all divisions and groups, leaving only the team structure.

In 1996, the museum implemented a guest services program. In 1994, the ad hoc facilities planning team recognized the current gallery management system was not working. At the time, they recommended implementing TQM more rapidly, developing staffing patterns that were more functional and less traditional, and developing an interpreter program.[67] Guest services used these recommendations to develop the host program. Guest services encompassed all areas of the museum that had daily contact with visitors or "guests," including admissions, gallery attendants, food services, museum stores, security, and facilities. The goal of the program was to create a memorable experience and "ensure there was one exceptionally high level of service from every museum staff member, regardless of their responsibilities."[68] This customer service model broached new territory for museums, and the Strong Museum looked outside the industry to benchmark best practices. The museum modeled many practices after Disney's customer relations, including holding all employees responsible for delivering an exceptional guest experience.

One of the guest service program's greatest challenges was that it was employee driven. In charging all employees to efficiently resolve guest problems, the institution trusted employees at all levels to make decisions that previously had been the purview of the supervisor. The boundaryless organizational structure made meeting high customer service standards an organization-wide task.[69] The program was supported by extensive employee training and dramatically increased in size and scope over time, developing as the mission evolved. This initial transition was difficult for some staff and particularly difficult for volunteers. In spite of training and coaching, staff and volunteers who did not transition into the guest services model or struggled to adjust to the new interactive design left the institution.[70]

1999–2003: The Search for a Unique Purpose

During the 1999 strategic planning process, the institution fully committed to a new, shared vision of interactive family programming. Having overcome attendance and community engagement concerns that motivated creation of the 1989 plan, institutional change was no longer driven by a goal as easily quantifiable as attendance, although numbers remained significant. While the desire to reach new audiences was sound business practice and still drove marketing efforts, the primary driving force for institutional change became the desire for the institution to serve a unique purpose. Given that the 1994 mission and resulting family-focused exhibits surpassed attendance projections, the Strong Museum undertook another market study in 1998. Results showed that with aggressive marketing, the Strong Museum could attract nearly 500,000 visitors annually with the current programming.[71] The atrium expansion success and new research "sparked plans to build 115,000 square feet of new space, renovate nearly 50,000 more, and raise the total square feet in the museum to 282,000."[72] The economic slump after September 11, 2001, delayed these plans.

In 2002, attendance had not yet reached 1998 projections, although membership had exceeded them, leading the Strong Museum to conduct another geodemographic survey. This study indicated that the Strong Museum had successfully reached all forty targeted groups identified in the 1998 survey, doubling the membership base and increasing attendance.[73] The Strong Museum had the potential to "win an audience of 763,048 visitors, and to attain a membership count of over 17,000 households within the 120-minute drive time market area" with a targeted and consistent marketing effort.[74] This research provided critical information for future programming by revealing that the population of children twelve and under had declined. The Strong Museum's focus demographic was shrinking, and to be successful, they would have to capture twelve- to eighteen-year-olds as well as other age groups.[75]

During the implementation of the 1999 strategic plan, the Strong Museum became even more interactive and family focused. This was the first strategic plan to list core values developed by staff: respect, focus, excellence, community, and fun, and the accompanying vision statement mentioned fun and play more prominently.[76] The plan focused on further developing educational programs and was guided by an internal document created in 1996, *Framework for Education*, which emphasized "the personal aspect of learning."[77] The learner-centric educational philosophy guided the education team as they reconstructed programs and led to adoption of Howard Gardner's theory of multiple intelligences in 1999.

Early in 2002, the Strong Museum published an internal document called *A Framework for Interpreting Play*. At this point, the institution was

considering including the cultural history of play as the fourth interpretive theme. According to Scott Eberle, Vice President for Interpretation,
the proliferation of children's museums demonstrated the audience appeal of play, and the interdisciplinary increase in play scholarship gave
the subject new depth.[78] The Strong Museum would finally be able to
"capitalize intellectually and programmatically on the true core of its
collections—all those dolls, toys, and other artifacts of play."[79] In addition, children and adults learn through play, and as an interpretive focus,
play complemented the theory of multiple intelligences and promoted
the institution's core values.

Around this time, the institution considered developing a national toy
hall of fame to recognize toys based on their historical and cultural significance but found that one had been established in 1998 in Oregon, at AC
Gilbert Discovery Village.[80] After an off-site presentation in 2002, a repre-
sentative of Discovery Village approached Adams and proposed the
Strong Museum purchase the National Toy Hall of Fame (NTHoF).[81]
Adams took this proposal to the trustees in July 2002, and the idea was
introduced and approved in the same meeting. The purchase provided
an opportunity to further a strategic plan objective and the possibility
that play would become an official interpretive theme.

In early 2003, Eberle and Adams realized that the cultural history of
play could be the museum's primary focus.[82] Trustees created a "play
study team" of board and staff members to explore the idea. The work of
the committee was critically important, with a potential impact that "ri-
vals both the founding of the museum and the shift toward a family and
child orientation."[83]

The study revealed four important observations. First, the collections
supported play. Staff discovered the original consultants had considered
play as a possible interpretive theme, and an analysis of each subset of
the collection determined that the collections did indeed support play.[84]
Second, school and public programs embraced play. By enlarging the role
of play, the educational team would be a resource for community educators.[85] Third, play was a growing field, and there were many groups
nationally and internationally that studied the role of play in society. At
the same time, no other museum made the study of play a primary focus.[86] Finally, play could make the Strong Museum a national institution.
For the last six years, the institution was marketed as a museum of creativity, exploration, play, and fun. By adopting a play mission, the Strong
Museum would refine its identity and enhance brand recognition, there-
by increasing visibility locally and nationally.[87]

In September 2004, the institution hosted an event with the theme
"new light about what Margaret Strong had in mind" and announced the
new mission to the public: "As an educational institution focused on
American cultural history, Strong Museum explores play in order to encourage learning, creativity, and discovery." The institution's vision

moved play to the forefront: "Strong Museum is the most exciting museum on the planet! We're a playful organization, but we're not fooling around." The play mission allowed the Strong National Museum of Play[88] to be a critical community resource by providing a "place where parents of younger children could go in a safe, clean, and family friendly environment . . . [where] meaningful learning took place but it was couched as fun . . . [with] world class exhibits that encourage children to touch things."[89]

2004–2007: Adjusting and Refining Mission Services

The strategic plan approved in 2004 refined the newly adopted mission and implementation methods. Now that the Strong National Museum of Play had an identity that served the community and fit the collections, it had to enhance institution offerings to reflect the changes. To incorporate dynamic exhibition structures to meet the mission, the Strong National Museum of Play expanded the facility. In 2004, the museum broke ground on a $37 million expansion that brought the museum's footprint to 282,000 square feet. This expansion included HVAC facilities, caterpillar atrium, Dancing Wings Butterfly Garden, a new gallery wing, education facilities, collections storage, and 1,000-gallon aquarium.[90]

In July 2006, after temporarily closing to complete construction, the museum officially reopened to the public as the Strong National Museum of Play and National Toy Hall of Fame. New exhibits embodied the new mission and "seamlessly blend collections and interactivity."[91] Some exhibits had more appeal to younger children, like *Reading Adventureland*, an exhibit that explored children's literature genres and allowed children to discover artifacts in the process. Others appealed more to older audiences and families but still encompassed the same level of interactivity. Along with additional interpretive space, the museum added two gift shops and an expanded food court to lengthen guest visits and increase the average dollar spent per visitor. The expansion proved to be a successful educational, marketing, and business tool. Prior to expanding, attendance peaked in 2001 at 393,749 visitors but leveled off at 340,000 for the following four years.[92] Even with the museum closed for forty-five days, attendance in 2006 reached 439,644, nearly an additional 100,000 visitors from the previous year.[93]

In focusing the mission on the core collection of dolls and toys, the Strong Museum sought a way to interpret its collection in a manner that was meaningful to the visitor. Adams and the trustees further demonstrated this intent by framing their desire to be critically important to the Rochester community through the questions, "What else can we do with the collections? What other interpretations and uses will they allow and support?"[94] As the community's needs evolved, the Strong National Museum of Play, firmly committed to a philosophy of continuous improvement, ongoing strategic planning, and a boundaryless organizational structure, continued to change.

CHANGE AS A CONSTANT, 2006–2010

Still operating under the 2004 strategic plan and extensions, the Strong National Museum of Play continued to refine the methods it used to deliver its mission to the community. The institution had been considering a formal education program since adopting the play mission, and members had been requesting it for quite a while.[95] In the fall of 2006, the Strong National Museum of Play welcomed fifty-six three- and four-year-olds to Woodbury Preschool. The newly expanded facility provided the space and excitement to capitalize on the new project. The preschool used Howard Gardner's theory of multiple intelligences and the Reggio Emilia model, which promotes respect, responsibility, and community through exploration and discovery in a learner-centric curriculum.[96] Woodbury Preschool furthered the mission by providing a place for children to learn through long-term, play-based experiences. The school modeled effective learning and teaching strategies, provided research opportunities for play-based learning scholars, and raised awareness of the importance of play in the school setting.[97]

At a November 2006 board meeting, Adams used TQM brainstorming techniques to lead a discussion about making the Strong National Museum of Play a national institution. From the outset, the trustees wanted the museum to be a national institution. Yet it took twenty-four years for the institution to find the mission and broad audience appeal to warrant such a consideration. In Adams's exercise, the board identified characteristics of national institutions. Authority emerged as the key variable. The Strong National Museum of Play would be a national institution when it became a recognized authority on play.[98] The museum would gain more authority by focusing on its educational mission. With previous motivating factors toward transformative change reached, developing authority and expanding the museum's national presence became a key goal at the Strong National Museum of Play and a driving force for change. This was reflected in the 2010 vision statement and in the 2010 strategic plan, interpretive programs, and marketing goals.[99]

To develop the authority necessary for national recognition, the National Museum of Play developed new avenues to deliver the mission to expanded audiences. Play as a topic appealed to children and families in execution and to scholars and educators in theory. In 2007 and 2008, the National Museum of Play launched two programs designed to further its scholarly audience. The first was opening the Brian Sutton-Smith Library and Archives, an onsite research library dedicated to the study of play.

Brian Sutton-Smith, a prominent American play theorist who worked to uncover the cultural significance of play in human life, donated over 2,500 books on play and his personal papers, and he agreed to become a "scholar-in-residence" at the museum. [100] The second was the 2008 launch of the *American Journal of Play*, a peer-reviewed forum that discussed the history, science, and culture of play, overseen by an editorial advisory board of twenty-five play scholars. In 2011, full issues of the journal were made available free online to maximize the publication's audience. Through Sutton-Smith's endorsement and the scholarly journal, the National Museum of Play gained substantial credibility with play scholars.

In 2009, the National Museum of Play again worked to expand its audience, this time to video game enthusiasts. The institution collected and studied video games, having recognized that electronic games "were changing the way people play, learn, and interact with each other." [101] Adams, inspired by the National Toy Hall of Fame's success, proposed the National Center for the History of Electronic Games (NCHEG). [102] After recognizing that electronic games are international commodities, NCHEG quickly became the International Center for the History of Electronic Games (ICHEG). ICHEG is currently the largest and most comprehensive collection of electronic games and materials. [103]

Through these developments, the Strong National Museum of Play provided a variety of services that catered to multiple audiences: families through the National Museum of Play and the National Toy Hall of Fame, scholars through the *Journal of Play* and Brian Sutton-Smith Library and Archives, and electronic gaming enthusiasts through the International Center for the History of Electronic Games. These audiences required different marketing techniques, and in 2010, the Strong National Museum of Play became the Strong and Play Partners. The Strong recognized that its marketing potential diminished greatly by trying to sell the National Museum of Play to someone interested in gaming. By using the Strong as the umbrella name, the institution could direct programs and services from each play partner to its intended audience while keeping them connected if any audience wanted to understand how they interact to meet the institution's mission and vision. [104]

At first, some members of the community found the new umbrella organization name "the Strong" confusing, given that the Strong Memorial Hospital (also located in Rochester, New York) is often referred to by the same name. At the same time, the rebrand successfully leveraged the Strong outside of Rochester and brought the institution new audiences from across the country. [105] The Strong's entrepreneurial approach, characterized by a philosophy of continuous change, ongoing strategic planning, use of marketing research, boundaryless organizational structure, and commitment to meeting the needs of the community, had paid off. Just a few months after rolling out the new brand, the board of trustees noted that with the "authority achieved through collections, mission, facilities, exhibits, and programs, research, publications, media coverage, and media recognition," the Strong had achieved national status. [106]

NOTES

1. Carol Sandler, *Margaret Woodbury Strong, Collector* (Rochester: The Strong Museum, 1989), 8.
2. Tour of the Strong, October 18, 2011.
3. "Margaret Woodbury Strong," http://www.thestrong.org/about-us/margaret-woodbury-strong.
4. *A Report to the Executors and Trustees of the Estate of Margaret Woodbury Strong on the Economic Experience of Privately Supported American Museums with a Special Section on Rochester Museums* (Rochester: Brian Sutton-Smith Archives, May 1, 1973).
5. William T. Alderson, "Right from the Start: The Strong Museum Opens Its Doors," *Museum News* (November/December 1982), 51. The quantified categorization of Mrs. Strong's collection is intended to give the reader an idea of its size and scope. Please note that while Margaret Strong's collection was estimated to be 300,000 objects at the time of her death, the categorization occurred across the next decade, after the museum had already begun to deaccession duplicates and non-museum-quality pieces; 65,000 items had been deaccessioned by the museum's opening (according to an AAM accreditation application completed by William T. Alderson in 1983).
6. Sandler, *Margaret Woodbury Strong*, 14.
7. Holman J. Swinney, *Report to the Board of Trustees of Margaret Woodbury Strong's Museum of Fascinations* (Rochester: Brian Sutton-Smith Archives, 1971).
8. Swinney, *Report to the Board of Trustees.*
9. Swinney, *Report to the Board of Trustees.*
10. Swinney, *Report to the Board of Trustees.*
11. E. McClung Fleming, *Report on Visit to the Strong Museum March 25–26* (Rochester: Brian Sutton-Smith Archives).
12. Holman J. Swinney, *The Strong Museum: Statement of Purpose* (Rochester: Brian Sutton-Smith Archives, 1973).
13. Minutes, the Strong Museum Board of Trustees (Rochester: Brian Sutton-Smith Archives, October 1973).
14. Remington Stockdale, Inc., letter to Holman J. Swinney, October 1976 (Rochester: Brian Sutton-Smith Archives).
15. Alderson, "Right from the Start," 52.
16. Tracey Linton Craig, "Going Strong," *History News*, January 1983, 10.
17. Linton Craig, "Going Strong."
18. William T. Alderson, Accreditation Application (Rochester: Brian Sutton-Smith Archives).
19. Attendance figures provided by G. Rollie Adams, the Strong, October 2011.
20. William T. Alderson, letter to Ms. Claire Sawyers (Rochester: Brian Sutton-Smith Archives, October 17, 1983).
21. Attendance figures provided by G. Rollie Adams.
22. William T. Alderson, letter to Mr. LaRoy B. Thompson (Rochester: Brian Sutton-Smith Archives, May 1, 1984).
23. Alderson's visiting committee consisted of Willard L. Boy (Field Museum of Natural History), James Morton Smith (Winterthur Museum and Gardens), Mildred S. Compton (Children's Museum of Indianapolis), Crawford Lincoln (Old Sturbridge Village), and Thomas Schlereth (professor of American studies at Notre Dame).
24. Minutes, June 1984.
25. Warren Leon, "The Margaret Woodbury Strong Museum: A Review," *American Quarterly* 41, no. 3 (September 1989): 532.
26. Board Minutes (Rochester: Brian Sutton-Smith Archives, May 1984).

27. Attendance figures provided by G. Rollie Adams.

28. Marie Hewett, "Developing Strong Evaluation Efforts," *Journal of Museum Education* 12, no. 1 (Winter 1987): 18.

29. Junior League, "Children's Museum Project," March 20, 1986, letter detailing results from January 1986 survey. The survey had only 279 respondents, and the letter does not say how the sample was selected.

30. While the gap in programming was acknowledged in board meetings, prior to the Junior League survey there were not recorded discussions about filling this gap.

31. W. T. Alderson, memo to Marie Hewett, "Plan of Action for Exhibit and Program Ideas Related to Young Children" (Rochester: Brian Sutton-Smith Archives).

32. Board Minutes (Rochester: Brian Sutton-Smith Archives, March 1987).

33. Hewett, "Developing Strong Evaluation Efforts," 18.

34. Jack Garner, "Little Hands on History," *Democrat and Chronicle*, October 8, 1987 (Rochester: Brian Sutton-Smith Archives).

35. Attendance numbers, the Strong.

36. G. Rollie Adams, internal memorandum (Rochester: Brian Sutton-Smith Archives, October 19, 1987).

37. G. Rollie Adams, interview by author, digital file (Rochester: Brian Sutton-Smith Archives, December 12, 2011).

38. For the purpose of clarity, plan extensions have been grouped with their original plan.

39. Adams, interview by author.

40. Adams, interview by author.

41. 1989 Strategic Plan.

42. Scott Eberle, interview by author through e-mail. December 2011.

43. Adams, interview by author.

44. Scott Eberle and G. Rollie Adams, "Making Room for Big Bird," *History News* (Autumn 1996): 25.

45. Attendance figures provided by G. Rollie Adams, the Strong (October 2011).

46. Board Minutes (Rochester: Brian Sutton-Smith Archives, May 1984).

47. The Winters Group, 1992 Market Study (Rochester: Brian Sutton-Smith Archives, 1992), 15.

48. The Winters Group, 1992 Market Study, 18.

49. Strong Museum 1993 Strategic Plan (Rochester: Brian Sutton-Smith Archives).

50. ArtsMarket, 1994 Market Survey (Rochester: Brian Sutton-Smith Archives, 1994).

51. ArtsMarket, 1994 Market Survey, 1.

52. ArtsMarket, 1994 Market Survey, 3.

53. Strong Museum 1994 Strategic Plan (Rochester: Brian Sutton-Smith Archives).

54. Adams, interview by author.

55. Board Minutes (Rochester: Brian Sutton-Smith Archives, January 1995).

56. G. Rollie Adams, memo, "Changing Our Approach to Exhibitions" (Rochester: Brian Sutton-Smith Archives, April 5, 1994).

57. Eberle and Adams, "Making Room for Big Bird," 25.

58. ArtsMarket, 1994 Market Survey.

59. Attendance figures provided by G. Rollie Adams, the Strong (October 2011).

60. Membership figures provided by G. Rollie Adams, the Strong (October 2011).

61. Adams, interview by author.

62. Board Minutes (Rochester: Brian Sutton-Smith Archives, April 1994).

63. Adams, interview by author.

64. A boundaryless organization structure is one that operates outside of the traditional vertical or silo-style hierarchy. The Strong Museum embraced the phrase, coined by Jack Welch, years after they were already operating in the boundaryless fashion.

65. Adams, interview by author.

66. G. Rollie Adams, "How Strong Museum Evolved into a Boundaryless Organization," presentation to the American Association of Museums Annual Meeting, May 18, 2000 (Rochester: Brian Sutton-Smith Archives).

67. Ad Hoc Facilities Planning Team, *Interim Report and Recommendations* (Rochester: Brian Sutton-Smith Archives, June 20, 1994).

68. Rich Battle, interview by author, digital file (Rochester: Brian Sutton-Smith Archives, October 19, 2011).

69. Kathie Dengler, interview by author.

70. Kathie Dengler, interview by author.

71. ArtsMarket, 1998 Market Survey for the Strong (Rochester: Brian Sutton-Smith Archives, 1998).

72. G. Rollie Adams, "Finally! A Museum of Play," *History News* (Summer 2006): 10.

73. 2002 Market Survey (Rochester: Brian Sutton-Smith Archives), 1.

74. 2002 Market Survey, 2.

75. 2002 Market Survey, 19.

76. 1999 Strategic Plan (Rochester: Brian Sutton-Smith Archives, 1999).

77. "Framework for Education" (Rochester: Brian Sutton-Smith Archives), 1996.

78. "Framework for Education."

79. Scott Eberle,"The Transforming Power of Play," *Journal of Museum Education* 33, no. 3 (Fall 2008): 269.

80. Board Minutes (Rochester, NY: Brian Sutton-Smith Archives, July 2002).

81. Adams, interview by author.

82. Adams, interview by author.

83. Play Study (Rochester: Brian Sutton-Smith Archives, 2003).

84. *Correlating Strong Museum Collections to Play*, Play Study (Rochester: Brian Sutton-Smith Archives, 2003).

85. Joann Hoffman, *How Making the Cultural History of Play the Central Focus of Strong Museum Will Impact the Museum's School and Public Programs*, Play Study (Rochester: Brian Sutton-Smith Archives, 2003).

86. G. Rollie Adams, *Some Background Regarding the Study of Play at Strong Museum*, Play Study (Rochester: Brian Sutton-Smith Archives, 2003).

87. Laura Sadowski, *How Making Play the Central Focus of Strong Museum Will Impact the Museum's Marketing Efforts*, Play Study (Rochester: Brian Sutton-Smith Archives, 2003).

88. Starting in 2003, the museum's official name changed to Strong National Museum of Play, although in minutes and memos the staff often continued to refer to the institution as Strong Museum.

89. Battle, interview by author.

90. Neil Kotler, Philip Kotler, and Wendy Kotler, "Model Museum Practice: The Strong National Museum of Play," in *Museum Marketing and Strategy*, 2nd ed. (San Francisco: Jossey-Bass, 2008), 112.

91. Adams, "Finally a Museum of Play!," 10.

92. Attendance figures provided by G. Rollie Adams (October 2011).

93. Ibid.

94. Adams, interview by author.

95. Joan Hoffman, interview by author, digital file (Rochester: Brian Sutton-Smith Archives, October 11, 2011).

96. "Woodbury PreSchool," the Strong, accessed February 11, 2012, http://www.museumofplay.org/education/woodbury-preschool.

97. Board Minutes, May 2005 (Rochester: Brian Sutton-Smith Archives).

98. Board Minutes, November 2006 (Rochester: Brian Sutton-Smith Archives).

99. 2010 Strategic Plan (Rochester: Brian Sutton-Smith Archives).

100. Board Minutes, February 2007 (Rochester: Brian Sutton-Smith Archives).

101. G. Rollie Adams, conversation with author (March 2012).

102. G. Rollie Adams, conversation with author (March 2012).

103. "About," the Strong, accessed February 11, 2012, http://www.icheg.org/about.

————. Board Minutes. Rochester: Brian Sutton-Smith Archives, 1970–2010.

————. *Bylaws of the Margaret Woodbury Strong Museum*. Rochester: Brian Sutton-Smith Archives, October 2004.

————. "Correlating Strong Museum Collections to Play." *Play Study*. Internal document. Rochester: Brian Sutton-Smith Archives, 2003.

————. *Education Division Notes for Board Meeting*. Rochester: Brian Sutton-Smith Archives, 1987.

————. *Framework for Education*. Internal document. Rochester: Brian Sutton-Smith Archives, 1996.

————. *How the Strong Is Organized*. Rochester: Brian Sutton-Smith Archives, August 2011.

————. *Interim Report and Recommendations of the Ad Hoc Facilities Planning Team*. Internal document. Rochester: Brian Sutton-Smith Archives, June 20, 1994.

————. Membership Figures. Provided by G. Rollie Adams, October 2011.

————. *One History Place Script*. Rochester: Brian Sutton-Smith Archives, August 1987.

————. *Operating Teams*. Rochester: Brian Sutton-Smith Archives, August 2011.

————. Press Releases. Rochester: Brian Sutton-Smith Archives, various dates.

————. *Rebranding Initiative Announced by Strong National Museum of Play*. Press release. Rochester: Brian Sutton-Smith Archives, September 2010.

————. "Some Questions and Answers about Why Strong Is Changing Its Interpretive Focus." *Play Study*. Internal document. Rochester: Brian Sutton-Smith Archives, 2003.

————. *Stabilizing Humanities Collections Institution: The Strong Museum*. National Endowment for the Humanities Sample Application Narrative. http://www.neh.gov/files/strong2006.pdf.

————. Strategic Planning Documents. Rochester: Brian Sutton-Smith Archives, various years.

————. Guided Tour. October 18, 2011.

————. *Untitled Museum Book*. Manuscript internally published in honor of a trustee. Rochester: Brian Sutton-Smith Archives, 2010.

————. Website. http://www.thestrong.org.

————. *1992 Visiting Committee Report*. Rochester: Brian Sutton-Smith Archives, 1992.

————. *1986 Results from the Junior League's Children Museum Project*. Internal memorandum. Rochester: Brian Sutton-Smith Archives, March 20, 1986.

————. *1992 Facility Utilization Study*. Rochester: Brian Sutton-Smith Archives, 1992.

————. *1994 Facilities Planning Team Notebook*. Internal documents. Brian Sutton-Smith Archives, 1994.

Swinney, Holman J. Professional Papers. Written correspondence, internal memoranda, and documents. Rochester: Brian Sutton-Smith Archives.

————. *Report to the Board of Trustees of Margaret Woodbury Strong's Museum of Fascinations*. Rochester: Brian Sutton-Smith Archives, 1971.

Weil, Stephen E. "From Being about Something to Being for Somebody: The Ongoing Transformation of the American Museum." *Daedalus* 128, no 3 (Summer 1999): 229–58.

————. "The Museum and The Public." *Journal of Museum Management and Curatorship* 16, no. 3 (1997): 257–71.

Welsh, Peter C. Letter to Holman J. Swinney. Rochester: Brian Sutton-Smith Archives, February 23, 1973.

Winters Group. *Study of Children's Activities, Final Report*. Rochester: Brian Sutton-Smith Archives, 1992.

SIX

Cultural Entrepreneurship

Case Discussion and Conclusions

Lynne A. Sessions

A small government-funded tourism center in Canada. Three badly damaged historic houses slated for urban renewal in an impoverished neighborhood in Brooklyn, New York. An aging vaudeville house turned theater in the Capital Region of upstate New York. A county historical society in the heartland of the United States. A vast collection of dolls, toys, and small items and an estate in Rochester, New York. What do these diverse situations have in common? What can they tell us individually and as a whole about cultural entrepreneurship, leadership, organizational change, vision, relevancy, and sustainability?

We begin by looking at what cultural entrepreneurship is. Recall that the Institute for Cultural Entrepreneurship (ICE) defines a cultural entrepreneur as a risk taker who can lead fundamental organizational change through powerful ideas and creative solutions. The entrepreneur identifies opportunities in change, takes calculated risks, and creates organizational infrastructures that not only quickly respond to change but are an integral part of the opportunity discovery process.[1] Creative entrepreneurial thinking and action yields sweeping change in organizational structure, identity, relevancy, and sustainability.

The organizations featured in the cases in this book differ in size, location, and type (historical house, arts organization, tourism center, collections-based museum). Founding stories differ. For example, the Centre d'histoire de Montréal was founded and funded by the Montreal city government. The Strong, founded out of Margaret Strong's substantial estate, began life well funded while the Weeksville Historical Society's impoverished beginnings mirrored the circumstances of the surrounding community. Yet when we view the cases through the definition and impact of cultural entrepreneurship, their organizational journeys, helmed by entrepreneurial leaders, are striking in their similarities. Each organization had one or more conditions that fostered the introduction of the entrepreneur to the organization. Once in place, the leaders found opportunities in complex environments and took calculated risks to capitalize on those opportunities. They developed creative solutions to problems and changed the structure of their organizations to implement those solutions. Most importantly, these efforts created a new vision for their respective organizations. Taken collectively, these leaders dramatically transformed their organizations, yielding powerful outcomes for the organization and the surrounding community. The following discussion addresses these similarities in greater detail.

INITIAL CONDITIONS FOR CHANGE

In writing about change in history organizations, Candace Matelic defines opportunities as conditions that facilitate change, that is, if the condition exists, it is easier to effect organizational change. She identifies a number of these conditions, including crisis and unstable environment, decline in attendance and financial support, support for experimental programs, expansion of collections or facilities, strong support for a new direction, a new director with a mandate and support for change, and what Matelic calls an "effectiveness paradigm," a focus on long-term qualitative outcomes rather than short-term focus on quantitative outcomes such as attendance, budget, and the bottom line.[2] These conditions can serve as a catalyst—a wake-up call for existing organizational leadership—and create opportunities for entrepreneurs to take root.[3] A number of these facilitating conditions for change are apparent in the five cases.

The resignation, retirement, or death of a leader or founder can represent a crisis that creates both internal and external instability through disruption of organizational operations and loss of institutional memory, organizational identity, and relationships with important external stakeholders, including funding sources. In these situations, the new leader is often given a powerful mandate by the board to effect change. The entrepreneur finds ways to capitalize on this opportunity.

For example, Pamela Green was hired in the wake of the retirement of Weeksville Historical Society founder and executive director Joan Maynard. In choosing Green, an outsider not only to the organization but also to the field, the board signaled openness to change and assigned a clear set of goals to be accomplished. Green seized the opportunity to lead a culture change at Weeksville Historical Society that better positioned the society for a sustainable future.

Philip Morris was hired after the passing of Proctors executive director Gloria Lamere. Lamere had stabilized Proctors's financial situation, which allowed the board to focus on the future. In hiring Morris, the search committee and board president wanted an executive director who could take Proctors to the next level and lead downtown development. Morris began his tenure with a powerful mandate for growth and community engagement.

G. Rollie Adams was hired after the resignation of Strong Museum executive director William Alderson. The trustees identified two major tasks for the new executive director: make the Strong Museum critically important in the community and begin strategic planning. When coupled with concerns for declining attendance and a mandate for community engagement that arose from *One History Place*'s success, Adams was well situated to create substantive change.

Concerns about financial support and attendance were also drivers for creating a climate conducive to entrepreneurial leadership at the Centre d'histoire de Montréal, Weeksville, and the Mississippi River Museum. For example, even though the Centre d'histoire was funded through the Montreal city budget, the museum needed to continually prove its value to ensure continued funding and support. Faced with two direct competitors and little repeat visitation to the museum, Director Jean-François Leclerc was continually rebuffed in his efforts to secure a larger portion of the city's cultural budget. The desire to expand funding was the driver that led to turning what had been a secondary market, residents of Montreal, into a unique, primary niche for the museum.

The Weeksville Heritage Center also struggled with declining financial support. Following the tragedy of the 9/11 attacks on the World Trade Towers, brand new executive director Pam Green found that the availability of funds from traditional sources had contracted substantially. She knew that the Weeksville Heritage Center would need to increase visibility, awareness, and impact in the community in order to attract new funding sources.

The Mississippi River Museum reassessed existing plans when attendance figures began to decline. The museum had completed a fund-raising effort to create an exhibition facility in a shared building with a riverboat casino. For the first time, expansion did not increase attendance. In fact, many of those visiting the casino were unaware of the museum. The board concluded that the high number of casino visitors had led the museum to "lose its sense of place." The failure of the expansion led the board to consider all museum offerings and resulted in rethinking the mission of the museum, setting the stage for the America's River Project.

Attendance concerns also galvanized the Strong, even before Adams's arrival. Less than two years after opening the museum, decreasing attendance had become a serious concern for the board. The years of research and inquiry that followed showed that there was a market for children-centered programming—which would ultimately lead to the restructuring of the Strong from a decorative arts museum to the National Museum of Play.

CREATIVITY, VISION, AND THE POWERFUL IDEA

Cultural entrepreneurs are able to connect the dots in ways that others, looking at the same situation, cannot. They find new ways to reach out to existing markets and bring in new markets. Philip Morris saw that Proctors could be used to drive economic development not just in Schenectady but in the entire Capital Region. He identified new revenue streams for Proctors that were remarkable because they derived from activities completely unrelated to the original mission of the theater. Selling heating and cooling, holding leases to encourage tenants to fill surrounding buildings, and providing garbage-compacting services for a fee benefited surrounding businesses and raised the attractiveness of the immediate area around the theater. Creative financing was used in multiple ways: funding educational programs through the BOCES system, leveraging historical tax credits through a partnership with Sherwin-Williams, and preventing the closing of Capital Rep, the local repertory theater. While others saw a depressed, empty city, Morris saw an opportunity.

Jerome Enzler saw opportunity in a potentially devastating development. The Mississippi River Museum was on its way to begin funding a major expansion only to find out that the City of Dubuque and the chamber of commerce had already begun planning for a major riverfront development project. Rather than oppose the city's plan, Enzler forged a lucrative partnership with both parties that would eventually revitalize the entire waterfront area and transform the Dubuque Historical Society's Mississippi River Museum into a national-caliber museum.

Pamela Green identified an unmet community need for fresh, healthy food. She brought students from the local school to Weeksville to learn about Weeksville's agricultural heritage through growing their own produce. The fresh, affordable produce was sold through a farmer's market to area residents. The project carried out the mission of Weeksville while improving the quality of life for neighboring residents. Jean-François Leclerc saw an untapped market and used ideas drawn from the health-care industry to gain access to that market by creating and implementing memory clinics. G. Rollie Adams saw the powerful potential of play as the central vision for the Strong.

CREATING ORGANIZATIONAL CHANGE

In order to carry out the vision, cultural entrepreneurs have to create organizational infrastructures that support the vision and are capable of responding to and creating change. This can mean changes in staffing, reporting relationships, day-to-day processes, marketing, and the board itself.

When Jean-Françoise Leclerc hired Catherine Charlebois to implement the memory clinics, her hiring was a signal to staff that things were changing. Later, as the Centre d'histoire pursued changing from a tourist center to telling the stories of the local community, new methods for gathering information from different groups were developed.

Pamela Green also made key staffing decisions. Given limited funding, she restricted hiring to filling positions in education and development, both of which were critical to increasing programming at Weeksville and raising needed funds. Green also worked to increase the size and diversity of the board. She implemented regular tour hours and new programs and discovered non-traditional funding sources. The change in mission was supported by a change in the organization's name and logo.

Like Green, Philip Morris also worked to restructure the board to bring in diverse skills and to support fund-raising. Morris restructured reporting relationships among staff, created new divisions, and encouraged the board to adopt a similar structure. He also upgraded technology, which improved organizational communication, provided information for better customer tracking, and became a source of revenue through offering technological services at a discounted rate to all of the tenants in the building.

Changes in organizational structure were a critical part of the transformation of the Strong. Adams eliminated divisions and created a team-based, boundaryless structure. The guest services program made each person in the organization responsible for responding to the needs of visitors. Guest services were benchmarked against Disney, and staff and volunteers received extensive training to meet high customer standards.

MANAGING RISK

Cultural entrepreneurs take and manage risks. But what exactly is risk? Everyone seems to have a different definition. A useful way to think about risk is to view it as a function of uncertainty. The greater the uncertainty about how expected outcomes may differ from actual outcomes, the greater the risk. The degree of risk affects the size of the payoff and the loss. For example, the interest rate that you earn on your savings account is low because there is very little uncertainty as to how expected outcomes may differ from actual outcomes. Banks in the United States are stable, and savings accounts are insured by the Federal Deposit Insurance Corporation (FDIC). When you process a withdrawal from your savings account, you are highly certain that your money will be available. To receive a higher return on your investment, you have to be willing to accept more risk. In making a decision about where to invest your money, you might try to reduce your risk by researching the opportunity, looking at economic trends, and considering the reputation of the bank or investment firm. You might even decide to experiment with a small investment to see what happens.

Cultural entrepreneurs do the same thing. Despite the stereotypical image of the "shoot from the hip" leader, entrepreneurs seek to manage risk through gathering information, experimenting, and assessing results. This information helps to reduce uncertainty and can be the impetus for the next round of identifying creative solutions for pressing problems. In addition to using consultants and conducting surveys, entrepreneurs seek to connect to their surrounding communities or stakeholders. Shirley Brice Heath notes that deep knowledge of relevant stakeholders provides the understanding necessary to address the stakeholders' problems.[4] Successful cultural entrepreneurs spend a great deal of time building community connections to develop the deep knowledge that provides the wellspring for creative solutions to problems, desires, and concerns that are relevant to their stakeholders. The cultural entrepreneurs featured in the cases all managed risk by gathering information, connecting with various stakeholders, and experimenting with new programs, assessing results, and making changes.

Jean-François Leclerc created relationships with individuals, neighborhoods, and other community partners. Pamela Green reassessed all existing programs against costs and as a result made changes to the Annual Family Day Festival. The July Salon Series, designed to introduce the community to emerging artists, underwent several transformations before arriving at its final form, an afternoon/early evening of relaxing music. Additional programs, symposia, and speakers' panels were also assessed. A geographic information system (GIS) study conducted by Proctors led to the conclusion that Proctors would need to become known as the arts and culture destination of the Capital Region. Proctors also interviewed regional leaders to determine fund-raising goals. Philip Morris regularly met with business leaders and city officials, and he sent his staff out into the community to learn about local residents' concerns. The Ambassador program was developed in response to this staff's fact finding. The Strong made extensive use of consultants and surveys to gather information. Program experimentation was reviewed against attendance and mission and adjusted accordingly.

Of the five featured cases, the America's River Project case best exemplifies the impact of community stakeholders on the development of the museum. Jerome Enzler developed and maintained an outstanding array of partnerships at the local, regional, state, federal, and national level. The extensive involvement of multiple stakeholders in the development and implementation of the America's River Project should serve as a model for all professionals working in cultural organizations.

RESULTS AND IMPACT

Ultimately, successful cultural entrepreneurs produce desired results. Traditionally, results have been measured by attendance (daily and program), membership, exhibition space, budget, and the bottom line. Not-for-profit cultural organizations, just like their for-profit counterparts, have to pay staff, the utility bills, and so on. If no one visits your museum (or buys your product), staying in operation will become increasingly difficult, if not impossible, to do. However, in today's complex and turbulent world, how do museums and other cultural institutions make sure that there is sufficient funding to "keep the lights on"?

In "The Relevant Museum: A Reflection on Sustainability," Emlyn Koster notes that the pursuit of relevancy can help museums achieve sustainability (defined as behavior that safeguards the well-being of future generations). Relevancy, or "relating to the matters at hand," correlates with eligibility for funding. Funding "keeps the lights on" and makes it possible for the organization to pursue its mission. In practice, this means that museums and other cultural organizations must "externalize" their actions by reaching out to stakeholders to change how they see the world and/or to improve their lives.[5] Successful cultural entrepreneurs create win-win solutions that improve the conditions of those in the community while contributing to the current and future financial health of the organization. We can see this being demonstrated by the entrepreneurs in the five cases.

The first memory clinic held by the Centre d'histoire de Montréal increased community awareness of the center. The Habitations Jeanne-Mance project increased community pride, and the first exhibition to use visual presentation based on oral history, *Lost Neighborhoods*, dramatically increased museum visitation. Jean-François Leclerc's vision led to development of new community partners, and the Centre d'histoire has become a place for Montreal residents to thoughtfully consider issues that affect their lives.

Pamela Green achieved the goals set for her by the Weeksville Historical Society's board of directors: restoring and opening the houses, funding and breaking ground on the cultural center, and building the infrastructure to support future society goals. But when talking with Green about success, she speaks of engaging people with programming, creating traveling exhibits, involving new funders, and empowering the community through, for example, the farmer's market that brings affordable, fresh food to those living in the food desert that surrounds Weeksville.[6]

Like Green, Philip Morris also accomplished the goals set out for him by the board of directors: complete the stage expansion project, upgrade technology, address staffing, and explore new opportunities. Under his leadership, Proctors became the largest cultural institution in New York State's Capital Region and a nationally known leader in art and culture. He used the financial power of Proctors as a driving force for economic revitalization of the Schenectady downtown area and the surrounding region. Morris expanded fund-raising capability by creating partnerships with other theaters, schools, and business partners and raised revenues by creating new products for new customers, for example, selling heating and cooling to surrounding businesses and offering a recycling center and garbage-compacting service. His creativity and inspired use of financial tools exemplified the aphorism, "A rising tide lifts all boats."

Jerome Enzler led a massive effort that transformed the Dubuque Historical Society, through the America's River Project, into the nationally known Mississippi River Museum. The museum and its partners raised $57 million for museum expansion and endowment and $131 million in leverage investments. The project revitalized the Dubuque riverfront with the addition of the Mississippi River Education and Conference Center, the Grand Harbor Resort and Indoor Water Park, the Mississippi River Walk, Greenways, Amphitheater, and supporting infrastructure. His leadership spurred the creation of partnerships and increased awareness and education along the entire length of the Mississippi River.

All of the organizations underwent mission changes, but the greatest transformational mission change took place at the Strong under the leadership of G. Rollie Adams. Through ongoing research and assessment that informed strategic planning, sweeping organizational structural change, building credibility with play scholars through an onsite library and a peer-reviewed journal, creating play partners like the International Center for the History of Electronic Games, and focusing on play and children through collections and exhibits that appealed to families, the Strong transformed from a decorative arts museum to the National Museum of Play. As a result, the Strong dramatically increased attendance while carving out a unique market niche.

CONCLUSIONS

Cultural entrepreneurs are risk takers who can lead fundamental organizational change through powerful ideas and creative solutions. The cases discussed here have shown a variety of individual leaders working in very different organizations who have indeed identified opportunities and created fundamental organizational change out of complex and turbulent environments. Some followed very structured processes characterized by ongoing strategic planning. Others developed opportunities and organizational change organically. In some instances, change occurred quickly, while for others, the process took years. Identifying the "big idea" wasn't enough. Organizational structures needed to be aligned with new missions that increased relevancy, and partnerships with stakeholders were vitally important to realizing sustainable results.

Clearly, cultural entrepreneurship is not a linear process. Choices and changes impact stakeholders, leading to new changes and opportunities. For those who seek to be more effective leaders, find creative solutions to problems, identify new opportunities, and build their organizations, we hope these cases and discussions will light a creative spark and provide insight into the actions of successful cultural entrepreneurs.

Pamela Green, Executive Director Emerita, Weeksville Heritage Center, offers these words of inspiration. "If you focus solely on challenges, you will not survive. Ask yourself, what is the benefit to the community? Do I believe in this project so strongly that I cannot be swayed? Am I willing to work really hard to realize this vision? Regardless of what common business practice dictates, you can move forward to achieve seemingly unachievable goals."[7]

NOTES

1. Entrepreneurial definitions drawn from the business literature include opportunity, uncertainty, and exposure to risk. More recently, the study of entrepreneurship is being applied to social innovation, creative industries, cultural organizations, and general not-for-profit organizations. Multiple and at times conflicting definitions abound. For our purposes, the definition used by the Institute for Cultural Entrepreneurship (ICE) encompasses the key components of entrepreneurship found in the business literature and applies those components to activities undertaken by not-for-profit museum, history, arts, and other cultural organizations.

2. Candace Tangorra Matelic, "Understanding Change and Transformation in History Organizations," *History News*, Spring 2008, 7–13. Additional conditions that facilitate change include staff salaries or benefits stable or declining, support for risk and shared power in decentralized structures, changing community, new expectations or lack of awareness or support for the organization, support for new professional initiatives, and a culture of learning.

3. One could argue that entrepreneurs may self-select into these situations, seeing the opportunity to effect organizational change through risk taking and creative problem solving.

4. Shirley Brice Heath, "Working with Community," in *Strategic Tools for Social Entrepreneurs: Enhancing the Performance of Your Enterprising Nonprofit*, ed. J. Gregory Dees, Jed Emerson, and Peter Economy (New York: Wiley, 2002), 141–60.

5. Emlyn Koster, "The Relevant Museum: A Reflection on Sustainability," *Museum News*, May/June 2006, 67–70, 85. This article contains a useful checklist for monitoring progress towards a goal of relevancy.

6. Lynne A. Sessions, interview with Pamela Green, May 2014.

7. Sessions, interview with Pamela Green.

BIBLIOGRAPHY

Heath, Shirley Brice. "Working with Community," in *Strategic Tools for Social Entrepreneurs: Enhancing the Performance of Your Enterprising Nonprofit*, edited by J. Gregory Dees, Jed Emerson, and Peter Economy, 141–60. New York: Wiley, 2002.

Koster, Emlyn. "The Relevant Museum: A Reflection on Sustainability." *Museum News*, May/June 2006, 67–70, 85.

Matelic, Candace Tangorra. "Understanding Change and Transformation in History Organizations." *History News*, Spring 2008, 7–13.

Index

About the Editors and Contributors

ABOUT THE EDITORS

Lynne Sessions holds an MBA in marketing from the University of Pittsburgh and a BS in business administration from Pennsylvania State University. Her career combines extensive experience in higher education with training and development and public relations experience in the not-for-profit sector. Throughout, she has specialized in bringing broad-based knowledge, experiences, and creativity to the strategic development of structures and processes designed to improve organizational performance. In 2005, her lifelong passion for the arts was realized when she created *Voice!*, an annual juried art exhibition sponsored by the Arc Otsego, which features work by artists with intellectual and other developmental disabilities from across New York State.

Gretchen Sullivan Sorin is director and distinguished professor at the Cooperstown Graduate Program, a museum studies program dedicated to the museum as a public service institution that must be entrepreneurial. She has worked for more than two hundred museums as a historian, exhibition curator, and strategic and interpretive planner and writes about African American history, art, and museums. Major exhibitions include: *Through the Eyes of Others: African Americans and Identity in American Art*; *In the Spirit of Martin: The Living Legacy of Dr. Martin Luther King, Jr.* for the Smithsonian Institution Traveling Exhibition Service; and *Bridges and Boundaries: African Americans and American Jews* for the Jewish Museum in New York City. Sorin is the author of *Touring Historic Harlem: Four Walks in Northern Manhattan* with Andrew Dolkart, *In the Spirit of Martin: The Living Legacy of Dr. Martin Luther King, Jr.*, and *Bridges and Boundaries: African Americans and American Jews*. She holds a BA from Rutgers University, an MA from the Cooperstown Graduate Program of SUNY College at Oneonta, and a PhD in history from the University at Albany.

ABOUT THE CONTRIBUTORS

Nicholas DeMarco studied history at the University at Albany and museum studies at the Cooperstown Graduate Program. He is now the de-

velopment associate at Barrington Stage, a not-for-profit professional theater company in the Berkshires. The case study on Proctors was developed for his master's thesis for the Cooperstown Graduate Program.

Jerome Enzler, a graduate of Loras College and the Cooperstown Graduate Program, is the president and CEO of the National Mississippi River
Museum and Aquarium and the National Rivers Hall of Fame. With
Enzler's guidance, the small Ham House Historical Society grew from a
budget of $13,000 in 1979 to $730,000 in 1989 and became a major mu-
seum/aquarium complex and revenue generator in the city of Dubuque
today. In 2013, Jerry Enzler was honored as a Champion of Change by the
White House for his time and effort in developing innovative ways to
help grow and expand the transportation industry.

Pamela Green is executive director emerita of the Weeksville Heritage
Center. She holds a master's degree in finance from the University of
Chicago and a bachelor's degree from Fisk University. Green joined the
Weeksville Heritage Center in 2001 and was responsible for building the
new education and cultural arts center, restoring the historic houses, and
establishing new programming, including a farmer's market. Before becoming director of Weeksville, Pam Green served as vice president of
outreach and strategic partnerships for Sesame Workshop. She was also a
founding member of the faculty of the Institute for Cultural Entrepreneurship and board vice president of MANY. Green retired from Weeksville in 2013.

Amy Hollister Zarlengo holds a BA degree from Lawrence University
and a master's degree from the Cooperstown Graduate Program. She has
worked as the projects coordinator at the Neil-Cochran House Museum
and currently serves as manager of corporate and foundation relations at
the Tacoma Art Museum. Zarlengo conducted research on the Strong
Museum for her master's thesis for the Cooperstown Graduate Program.